OFFICIALLY WITHDRAWN

P9-CAF-253

C. 2

791.43 Edelson, Edward
EDE
Great kids of the
movies

DATE			
NOV 26 '80	508	208	
DEC 10 '80	209	202	
	202	303	FEB 28 '8
DEC 17 '80	509	210	
MAR 31 '81	509	APR 26 '84	210
APR 20 '81	507	APR 23 '8	20 209
MAY 15 '81	202	MAY 17	204
MAY 29 '81	204		207
OCT 14 '81	209		
OCT 28	508		
	208		
JAN 7 '82	208		

LIBRARY
LONGFELLOW SCHOOL
BERKELEY CA

© THE BAKER & TAYLOR CO.

GREAT KIDS OF THE MOVIES

Other books by the author:

GREAT MONSTERS OF THE MOVIES

THE BOOK OF PROPHECY

VISIONS OF TOMORROW

FUNNY MEN OF THE MOVIES

GREAT MOVIE SPECTACULARS

TOUGH GUYS AND GALS OF THE MOVIES

GREAT KIDS
OF THE MOVIES

EDWARD EDELSON

Doubleday & Company, Inc.
Garden City, New York

791.43
Ede
C.r

The author thanks Paula Klaw of *Movie Star News* for assistance on this and other books.

LIBRARY
LONGFELLOW SCHOOL
BERKELEY, CALIF.

Library of Congress Cataloging in Publication Data

Edelson, Edward, 1932–
  Great kids of the movies.

  Includes index.
  1. Moving-picture actors and actresses—United States—Biography—Juvenile literature.   2. Children as actors—Juvenile literature.   I. Title.
PN1998.A2E27   791.43′028′0922 [B]
ISBN 0-385-14127-0 Trade
        0-385-14128-9 Prebound
Library of Congress Catalog Card Number 78–14697

Copyright © 1979 by Edward Edelson
All Rights Reserved
Printed in the United States of America
First Edition

CONTENTS

CHAPTER 1

Show Business

So you want to be a star.

Admit it, you do, deep down inside. There's hardly a kid alive who hasn't dreamed at one time or another of starring in a hit movie or being the lead on a smash television series. Just think of having your name up in lights, of people stopping you on the street to ask for your autograph, of the money rolling in, of big limousines and the applause of the crowds. Who wouldn't want all the glory and fun and money that comes from being a famous child actor?

There's a lot of truth in that glowing picture of show-business success. The old Hollywood dream of being just another kid on the block one day and being rich and famous almost overnight has come true over and over again. But there's also a dark side to the show-business story that shouldn't be forgotten by any kid who thinks that the world is just waiting to discover his or her talent and that fame is just around the corner.

To start with, most young actors and actresses who want to be stars don't make it. Show business is one of the most competitive fields on earth, and dozens of aspirants fail for every one who succeeds. A movie or television producer may audition scores or even hundreds of applicants before picking the one who finally gets the job. You read about the winners all the time in the newspapers and magazines, but you hardly ever hear about the ones who tried just as hard but didn't get the part.

Admittedly, the rewards for those who do make it can be fabulous. After Tatum O'Neal became a big hit in the movie *Paper Moon* at age eight, her father, actor Ryan O'Neal, insisted that she wasn't going to accept any more film parts. Then one day Tatum told her father that she wanted to use her movie earnings to buy a horse ranch. "You only made $16,000," said Ryan. "That won't buy it." Tatum went right back to work, getting a contract for *The Bad News Bears* that paid her $350,000 and nine per cent of the movie's net profits. That made her the highest-paid child star in the history of Hollywood. You can't make that kind of money delivering papers, baby-sitting, or working at the corner hamburger shop.

On the other hand, most child stars don't actually wallow in wealth. When Shirley Temple was the number-one box-office attraction in Hollywood, she was getting an allowance of just $4.25 a week. (But admittedly, money went a lot further in those Depression days.) By law, much of the money that a child actor earns must go into a trust for the adult years, a provision that was made necessary by the underhanded actions of some adults who had control of high-paid child stars in the past.

Then again, being a child star doesn't mean that you get out of going to school. Again by law, any child, however rich and famous, must get a minimum amount of schooling. In the good old days when Hollywood turned out hundreds of movies a year, several studios maintained schools on the lots so that child actors and actresses could go to classes between takes. Today, a child star might have a tutor, or maybe go to a private school. A lot of the time, neither of those alternatives is too great. Having a tutor means that you can miss out on a lot of the fun that most kids have, the fun of palling around with children your own age. Since acting can be a tough job requiring long hours under hot lights, a child star can be worn to a frazzle between lessons and scenes. And if you go to a private school, being a star might not make life too easy. There are plenty of envious kids around who are ready to make life a little miserable for anyone who is making it big in the acting world.

All in all, child acting is really a pressure-cooking existence. Moviegoers and television watchers generally like child stars who radiate innocence and geniality. But the same kid who looks so wide-eyed and happy on the screen may need a set of iron nerves to take the constant tension of being in the spotlight.

But the worst of it all is that child stars grow up. Growing up is inevitable, but it's bad in two ways for young actors and actresses. First of all, being a hit as a child is no guarantee at all of being a success as an adult actor. If you look at the record, you'll find that most child stars never made the transition to a satisfactory acting career when they outgrew their youthful charm. Sure, there are exceptions to that rule, but only enough exceptions to make the rule look good.

Sometimes a child's career can come to a sudden halt at a surprisingly young age. Consider Baby Le Roy, who starred in several comedies with W. C. Fields in the 1930s. (Supposedly, the irascible Fields mixed gin with his costar's orange juice one day, and then chortled in his wicked way when the tot kept falling asleep.) For all practical purposes, Baby Le Roy's acting career was over by the time he was six years old.

Admittedly, Baby Le Roy was an extreme case. Most child stars stay in the limelight for ten years or so. But there always comes that time when a child stops being a child and has to make it in the grown-up world. The sad truth is that most child stars don't make it in acting.

And the sadder truth is that many child stars learn that the life of a kid actor is not the best training for normal adult life. Just think of what it must be like to be in that position. Imagine that for years you've been used to making lots of money, being in the spotlight, being treated like a very special person. Then, just at the time when most people are starting to learn how to shoulder the burdens of being grown up, all of that is taken away from you. The money stops rolling in. The skills you were so proud of don't seem to matter any more. The people who used to recognize you on the street walk past you without a glance. Growing up is tough enough for an ordinary kid. It can be traumatic for a kid who has been a star.

The picture isn't all dark. There are plenty of success stories. Take Dickie Moore, one of the biggest child stars of the 1930s. Like so many other child actors and actresses of the time, Dickie Moore was a member of "Our Gang." Like many another child star, he got started young. In 1926, when he was one year old, Dickie made his first appearance in a movie; he was the baby who later grew up to be John Barrymore in a film called *The Beloved Rogue*. By the time he was seven, he had been in movies with Barbara Stanwyck, Marlene Dietrich, and other stars of that golden age. Dickie joined "Our Gang" in 1932 and was an instant hit.

He stayed with the "Our Gang" series for just one year, moving on to bigger things: the title role in *Oliver Twist* (1933) and juicy parts in *The Story of Louis Pasteur* (1935), *The Life of Emile Zola* (1937) many other films. Unlike many other child stars, Dickie Moore made the transition to older roles easily. As a teenager he played opposite Gary Cooper in *Sergeant York* (1941) and with Don Ameche in a delightful 1943 comedy, *Heaven Can Wait*. He also had the distinction of giving Shirley Temple her first screen kiss, in a 1942 film called *Miss Annie Rooney*.

The name "Dickie" was growing increasingly unsuitable for a strapping young man, and it was Dick Moore who went into wartime service with the Army. He was a reporter for the Army newspaper *Stars and Stripes*, worked briefly on a Los Angeles newspaper after the war, had a few more acting parts in movies (the last one was *Member of the Wedding*, made in 1952), and then went east to New York. Just as easily as he had become a movie star, Dick Moore be-

Dickie Moore with an animal friend in *Timothy's Quest*, which was made at the height of his success. (Paramount, 1936)

came a successful public relations executive, the head of his own company. He moved smoothly from childhood prosperity in the 1930s to adult prosperity in the 1970s.

But for every such happy Hollywood ending, there is a different, sadder story to be told. The life of another "Our Gang" star, Carl "Alfalfa" Switzer, is one such story. Alfalfa was the freckle-faced kid whose hair was parted in the middle and whose singing voice was delightfully squeaky. Carl and his brother Harold had made a few public appearances at entertainments in their Illinois home town, and when they went to visit their grandparents in California, they went to the Hal Roach Studios to see if they could crash show business. The story goes that they couldn't get past the guard at the gate, who was constantly besieged by aspiring child actors, and so they sneaked into the studio commissary and launched into their song-and-dance act. In one of those Hollywood twists, Hal Roach, the head of the studio, was eating in the commissary. He liked what he saw and signed the boys to contracts on the spot. (Things like that really happened in those days.)

Starting with *Beginner's Luck* in 1935, Alfalfa appeared in sixty-one "Our Gang" episodes over the next six years. (Harold had a much shorter career, being dropped after just a few episodes.) By that time, Alfalfa was thirteen years old and had outgrown "Our Gang." His earnings, which were $750 a week at the peak (an awful lot of money for those days) dropped precipitously. He did have the lead in a 1940 Republic movie called *Barnyard Follies*, but in a few years the best he could do was bit parts. He supplemented his acting income by serving as a hunting guide in the woods of northern California. There were a couple of brushes with the law, including a mysterious episode in which an unknown assailant shot him in the arm in 1948. At the beginning of 1959, Carl Switzer got into an argument with a partner of his about fifty dollars which Switzer claimed was owed to him. There was a scuffle, and a gun went off. Shot in the stomach, Carl Switzer was dead at the age of thirty-one. It was a tragic ending to a life that had started so sunnily.

Of course, it should be said that the lives of most child stars do not follow as sad a scenario as that of Alfalfa Switzer. The truth is that most child actors and actresses are pretty much like the rest of us when it comes to growing up. Some of them make it big in show business as adults. Some of them move on to success in other fields of life, often helped by the money that was put away for them when they were stars. Some of them run into serious trouble. And many of them become ordinary folks—salesmen, executives, farmers, housewives. There are occasional appearances on television talk shows, and now and then a nostalgic reunion with the Hollywood kids of yesteryear. But the big lesson that most child stars have to learn is that fame, however intoxicating it may be at the time, is fleeting.

So there it is, you would-be kid star. Breaking in is tough. Acting is hard work, and staying on top is difficult. You've got to grow up sooner or later, and that means facing a different kind of world than you've been used to. In short, there are about as many thorns as roses in this business of being a child star.

But is that kind of sensible talk going to discourage anyone? Of course not. The kid who lies awake in bed at night, dreaming of being the next Shirley Temple or Judy Garland or Tatum O'Neal, isn't going to be discouraged by mere reality. The thrill of stardom just won't go away, and the stories of kids who made it big are too exciting to ignore. After all, this would be a fairly dreary world if no one wanted to be a star.

LONGFELLOW SCHOOL LIBRARY
BERKELEY, CALIFORNIA

CHAPTER 2

Shirley and Judy and Mickey

It was an unbelievable story, one that Hollywood would have rejected indignantly if anyone had proposed it as a film script. In the 1930s Hollywood was in the heyday of one of its golden eras. The movie industry was awash with some of the greatest personalities in its history—Gable, Garbo, Dietrich, Cooper, Tracy, Hepburn, Cagney, Bogart, and dozens more. And sitting atop the heap, the biggest box-office draw on earth, was a curly-haired little girl who was less than four feet tall and had never taken an acting lesson in her life. Unbelievable.

The girl was Shirley Temple, and hers was a success story that still is without parallel in Hollywood history. No child star has ever had the impact that Shirley did, before or since. It is true that the story of Mary Pickford, "America's Sweetheart," is nearly as spectacular. In the earliest days of Hollywood, the days when film makers were just discover-

ing that there could be such a thing as a movie star, an actor
or actress who could draw people into the theater by the
sheer power of a name, Mary Pickford was one of the biggest names there was. But Mary Pickford achieved her
greatest success in her teens and even older. Shirley Temple
almost literally walked out of nursery school and into stardom.

The most amazing part of the story is how simple it all
seemed to be. Shirley never had to fight for anything that
came her way. She was born in Santa Monica, California,
within hailing distance of Hollywood, in 1928, the daughter
of a bank manager, George Temple, and his wife, Gertrude.
At the age of three, Shirley went to dancing school for lessons—something that a writer later described as "similar to
Lynn Fontanne going to a dramatic academy to take a
course in acting."

Before she was four years old, Shirley was discovered at
the dancing school by Charles Lamont, a director of a
second-line studio called Educational Pictures. She was in a
series called "The Baby Burlesks," and then moved into another called "Frolics of Youth." Her first notable feature film
was a 1934 musical titled *Stand Up and Cheer*. She
was an immediate hit and signed a seven-year contract with
Fox Productions, at a salary that seemed immense—$150 a
week.

Hollywood stars turned out movies at an assembly-line
rate in those days, and Shirley Temple was no exception.
She made nine films in 1934, four in 1935, four in 1936, and
two in 1937. By then, she was sitting firmly on top of all the
box-office popularity charts. She had also received a special

miniature Oscar in 1934 for bringing "more happiness to millions of children and millions of grownups than any child of her years in the history of the world." It was typical Hollywood talk, but it probably was nothing but the truth. Her original contract had been torn up and she was earning $1,500 a week (that went up to $300,000 a picture in 1939, at a time when a worker could support a family on $40 a week.) Even when Shirley was too young to read the scripts of the movies she acted in—she learned her lines by having her mother read to her at bedtime—she was the center of a remarkable cult.

There were Shirley Temple dolls and Shirley Temple dresses and Shirley Temple imitators galore. Every other studio in Hollywood felt that it had to have a singing, dancing moppet to match Shirley Temple. Literally thousands of kids auditioned for the spot, but none of them ever had the Shirley Temple charm.

The plots of her movies were not noted for originality. In most of them she was either an orphan who found a happy ending with a new family or the child of a single parent (widowed, of course, since Hollywood did not recognize the existence of divorce in those days) who found a new mate for her father or mother. There was always a pause for a song such as "On the Good Ship Lollipop" or "Animal Crackers in My Soup" or "What I Want for Christmas." In a number of her movies, she costarred with the great black dancer Bill "Bojangles" Robinson, who invariably played the old, faithful family servant. In the 1970s some of those movies seem racist; at the time they were made, they were in tune with the national mood.

Shirley Temple sings and dances with Bill "Bojangles" Robinson in *Rebecca of Sunnybrook Farm*. (Twentieth Century–Fox, 1938)

The curious thing about the Shirley Temple movies that were so popular at the time is how completely they have vanished today. Shirley Temple worked with some great directors, such as John Ford (for whom she made the Kipling classic *Wee Willie Winkie*) and some notable actors, such as Adolphe Menjou (with whom she made the Damon Runyon Broadway tale *Little Miss Marker*). But hardly anyone ever thinks of showing those films today. One will show up now and then on television, but the revival theaters that flourish in some cities usually manage to get along without Shirley Temple movies. Either the world is ignoring some good movie-making, or some good film fun has faded with time.

Eventually Shirley Temple grew up. Her story in later life is relatively smooth, but there were some bumpy spots along the way. Her contract with Twentieth Century–Fox ended in 1940, and she was cut loose by the studio without much sentimental reminiscing. In the hard world of Hollywood, the people who kept track of the money had noticed that her last few pictures were not nearly as successful as her earlier efforts.

Shirley moved over to MGM, where she made just one movie. Her career was not over, however; she signed with David O. Selznick and was successful in several films as a teenager: *The Bachelor and the Bobby-Soxer* (1947) with Cary Grant, *Fort Apache* (1948) with John Wayne, *Mr. Belvedere Goes to College* (1949) with Clifton Webb. At the age of seventeen she married John Agar, who had starred with her in *Fort Apache* and whose movie future seemed to be bright. But Agar's acting career fizzled out, and the marriage ended in divorce in 1949.

The next year she married Charles A. Black. As Shirley Temple Black, she has had a remarkably successful second career in politics and diplomacy. She lost in an effort to be elected to the House of Representatives as a Republican in California, but she was named ambassador to Ghana in 1974 (after serving in the United States delegation to the United Nations) and later was given the post of chief of protocol to President Gerald Ford.

When Mrs. Shirley Temple Black was given the Life Achievement Award of the American Center of Films for Children in 1977, it seemed almost surprising that this poised, beautiful woman of forty-nine had once been a curly-headed moppet who had tap-danced her way to stardom. Those who had been involved in films at the time were very much aware of what Shirley Temple had meant, but she herself said briskly, "I'm not sentimental about the past; the most important moment is now."

There was one curious sidelight to that 1977 award. It was also called the Ruby Slipper Award, a reference to the ruby slippers worn by a girl named Dorothy in the movie *The Wizard of Oz*. Hardly anyone today remembers that the role of Dorothy in that film was supposed to have gone to Shirley Temple. MGM, which was making *The Wizard of Oz*, offered to lend two of its biggest stars, Jean Harlow and Clark Gable, to Twentieth Century–Fox for Shirley's services. But Jean Harlow died tragically, and the deal was called off. Instead, MGM gave the role to another young actress, whose career, both in and out of the movies, was in striking contrast to that of Shirley Temple.

LONGFELLOW SCHOOL LIBRARY
BERKELEY, CALIFORNIA

The girl who got the starring role in *The Wizard of Oz* was born in 1922, with the name Frances Ethel Gumm, in Grand Rapids, Minnesota. Her parents, like Shirley Temple's, also had acting ambitions for their children, but there was no overnight discovery by a talent scout in Frances's case. She had to work her way up the hard way, first singing with her sisters on the stage of the small movie theater that their father owned, then going on a grueling vaudeville tour. The Gumm sisters were hardly one of the great hits of the day, but they kept at it.

Naturally the Gumm sisters and their parents ended up in Hollywood. But there was no overnight discovery and success of the kind Shirley Temple experienced. Instead, the Gumm family went through a routine that was more commonplace—a routine of hard work at ordinary jobs, of making any kind of theatrical appearance at any price in hopes that a talent scout would be there, of living dingy lives while dreaming of stardom. The Gumms did fairly well financially, but after five years all that the performing sisters had to show as far as movie experience went was a brief appearance in one film short.

The girls went back on the road, with mixed success. Finally a Hollywood agent named Al Rosen heard Frances sing and signed her up—except that he didn't sign Frances Gumm but Judy Garland. The new first name came from a favorite song, and the new last name was borrowed from a Chicago film critic.

By common agreement, young Judy Garland was a rather plain girl with a tendency to overweight. But she could sing like an angel. That voice got her a contract at MGM in 1934, when she was twelve years old. But she was still no over-

night success. There were plenty of other child actresses on
the MGM lot in those days, and Judy did not jump ahead of
the pack instantly. She was put on a strict diet to slim her
down (the commissary was told to feed her nothing but
chicken soup, no matter how much she pleaded for banana
splits) and was tried out in a short subject with another
aspiring young singer, Deanna Durbin, just to see how they
would look on film.

Both of them looked fine, and things began to happen.
Universal Pictures had a script called *Three Smart Girls*,
which required a popular singer, and the studio asked MGM
to lend Judy for the part. MGM said no. The script was
rewritten to fit in a classical singer, and Deanna Durbin got
the part—a part that sent her right into star billing. Judy, instead, went into a routine musical called *Pigskin Parade*,
which got her good, if not sensational notices, and into
Broadway Melody of 1938 (which was released in 1937),
where she was a smash hit crooning "You Made Me Love
You" to a picture of Clark Gable.

A few more routine musicals, straight off the big-studio
assembly line, followed. But the really big break came when
MGM couldn't get Shirley Temple for *The Wizard of Oz*.
Judy got the part, even though she was a blossoming sixteen
years old. The studio made special caps for her teeth,
strapped her into a corset that hid her figure, made her diet
even more strict, and turned her into eleven-year-old
Dorothy Gale of Kansas, who was carried away by a tornado
to marvelous adventures with the Tin Woodman, the Scarecrow, and the Cowardly Lion in the wonderful land of Oz.
The result was one of the best films ever made.

Based on a book by L. Frank Baum, *The Wizard of Oz*

Judy Garland in *The Wizard of Oz* with, from left to right, Jack Haley as the Tin Woodsman, Ray Bolger as the Scarecrow, Frank Morgan as the Wizard, and Bert Lahr as the Cowardly Lion. (MGM, 1939)

was—and is—perfect in almost every way. Judy captured every heart when she wistfully sang "Over the Rainbow"—a song that was very nearly cut out of the movie. British airmen fighting the Battle of Britain in 1940 made another song from the film, "We're Off to See the Wizard," their unofficial theme. Even today, four decades later, *The Wizard of Oz* has not aged a bit. It is shown once a year on television, and captures a huge audience every time. It will never grow old.

But Judy Garland was growing old, at least in movie terms. From playing a very young Dorothy Gale, she had to switch back to teenage roles. She did so successfully, but at a frantic rate. Those were the days when thousands of movie theaters across the country were greedy for new films, and the big studios worked their stars hard to meet the demand. With hardly a pause for rest, Judy was hurried into what seemed to be an endless series of musicals with Mickey Rooney, who was also a bright teenage star. The plots of the musicals often seemed interchangeable—the finale always seemed to be a musical show that Judy and Mickey put on to save the old homestead, the ranch, the theater, or anything else that the writers could think of—but the sheer expertise of Judy and Mickey, as well as the wealth of talent available to the studios, made the movies work.

But a legend began to grow about the toll that the making of those films took on young Judy Garland. There were stories which said that Judy lived on pills. According to those stories—whose truth is still being debated—Judy would be put to sleep at the end of a grueling day with sleeping pills and would be awakened with stimulants to prime her for another hard day before the cameras. Constantly hungry —the studio would not let up on her diet—always hard at work, Judy turned out a series of sunny, uncomplicated films —*Babes in Arms, Andy Hardy Meets a Debutante, Strike Up the Band, Little Nellie Kelly, Ziegfeld Girl, Life Begins for Andy Hardy, Babes on Broadway,* and so on. (Incidentally, all those films, as well as *The Wizard of Oz,* were made in exactly three years.)

Judy Garland went on to a great career as an adult musical star. But the legend of Judy Garland had nothing to do with those musicals. Her life turned out to be rather unhappy. There were constant rumors of drug use. She was married several times. Her movie career petered out (although her fans always filled the hall when she made personal singing appearances). Judy Garland died in 1969, tragically young, six years after she had made her last movie.

But the curious thing is this: Judy Garland, who had tough times for most of her life, lives on in the minds of her fans in a way that Shirley Temple, whose career was one of almost unbroken success, does not. If you look for books about Shirley Temple, you will find hardly one. But biographies of Judy Garland fill the shelves; sometimes it seems that a new one appears every month. *The Wizard of Oz* keeps coming back, while most of the Shirley Temple films remain in the vaults. Maybe it's the contrast between the bitterness of her real life and the image of Dorothy Gale of Kansas singing wistfully about that land over the rainbow, but whatever the reason, Judy Garland has achieved a kind of immortality that has come to only a few others, such as Humphrey Bogart.

———————

Mickey Rooney is a legend of a different kind. He has led the kind of life that they write show-business novels about.

He was born in Brooklyn in 1920 as Joe Yule, Jr., the son of parents who were in vaudeville. Before he was two years old, he crawled out on the stage during a performance, and was in the act after that. He had his first movie part, as a midget, by the age of four. Not long afterward, a studio announced that it was holding auditions for a series to be based on a character named Mickey McGuire, who was in the popular comic strip "Toonerville Trolley." In the strip, McGuire had black hair. Young Joe was a blond, but his stage-savvy mother used shoe polish to darken it and tugged him off to the audition. He got the role, and carried the Mickey McGuire series for six years. Largely because of him, the series was one of the few imitators of the popular "Our Gang" shorts that had any success.

For a while, his parents thought of changing his name to Mickey McGuire. Instead, they chose Mickey Rooney. It was a good idea, because the McGuire shorts were just the beginning. At an age when some child stars' careers were ending, Mickey was moving on to bigger things.

Before he was a teenager, he was starring in big-budget films. Among his odder roles was that of Puck, a blithe spirit, in the film version of Shakespeare's *A Midsummer Night's Dream*. In 1937 MGM had the idea of using Mickey in a film version of a domestic play about a typical American family named Hardy. That first film, titled *A Family Affair*, was so successful that it led to a long series of Andy Hardy features. Mickey played Andy, who was an almost painfully typical teenager. In *A Family Affair* Lionel Barrymore played Andy's father and Spring Byington his mother. For the rest of the Andy Hardy series the parents were played

The old image of the American teenager: Mickey Rooney and Judy Garland sip soda through a straw in *Babes on Broadway*. (MGM, 1941)

by two reliable members of the MGM stock company: Fay Holden was Andy's mother, and Lewis Stone played his father, Judge Hardy, who was always good for a stern but kind lecture when Andy went wrong out of sheer youthful spirits. Set in a typical American town called, believe it or not, Carvel, the Andy Hardy series went through a total of seventeen films in more than twenty years, earned $25 million for MGM, and featured, along the way, such talents as Judy Garland, Lana Turner, Esther Williams, and Susan Peters. The last Andy Hardy film was made in 1958, when it was clearly evident that Mickey Rooney could no longer pass for a teenager on the screen.

But Andy Hardy wasn't the only part that young Mickey played, by any means. He won a special Academy Award for playing a tough kid in *Boys' Town* (1938); he had the title role in *Young Tom Edison* (1940); he was impressive in the film version of William Saroyan's novel *The Human Comedy* (1943); he did those musicals with Judy Garland, and much, much more.

At the ripe age of twenty-eight, with a quarter century of show-business experience behind him, Mickey Rooney left off being a young actor and began being just an actor. His acting career as an adult continues to this day. His private life hasn't always been smooth—he is a short man who seemed to have a penchant for marrying tall women—but Mickey has bounded through life with the endless energy that he showed from the start. Appearing in everything from tired comedies (*Francis in the Haunted House,* a 1956 film featuring a talking mule) to serious dramas (*The Bold and the Brave,* another 1956 film, for which he won an Academy

Award nomination), Mickey Rooney has always given a good show.

Early in 1978, Mickey told reporters that he was going to retire after he finished the film he was then making. His agent told the press, in effect, not to pay any attention; he said that Mickey always talked about retiring when he was in the middle of a film, and always changed his mind when the next movie part came along. For all we know, the ageless kid called Mickey Rooney might go on forever.

CHAPTER 3

The Girls in the Gang

The 1930s were the heyday of the young actor in Hollywood. When Judy Garland was at MGM, for example, she
went to classes in the studio school with such as Mickey
Rooney, Ann Rutherford, Lana Turner, Freddie Barthole-
mew, Jackie Cooper, and a few others. Kids were big box-
office potential, and every studio had to have its stable of
fresh-faced boys and girls who radiated wholesomeness and
who could also cry on cue, if desired. Those were innocent
times, and sweetness and light were in style.

One big exception to that rule was a not especially beautiful screen brat named Jane Withers. Born in Atlanta in
1926, pushed ahead in her acting career by an ambitious
mother, Jane was out in Hollywood by the age of six. After
two years of bit parts, she struck it rich in a 1934 Shirley
Temple movie, *Bright Eyes*. Shirley played the good little

That's Jane Withers in glasses, casting a skeptical eye at Shirley
Temple in *Bright Eyes* (Twentieth Century-Fox, 1934)

girl, of course, and Jane Withers played a nasty, kicking, bit-
ing tomboy. In the course of the film Jane kicked Shirley,
asked Santa Claus for a real machine gun (and fired a toy
gun at Shirley when the real gun was not under the tree),

and roughed up little Miss Temple mercilessly. The audience loved it.

From then on, Jane Withers was a star. By 1937 she was number seven in a poll of favorite box-office attractions and was earning around $2,000 a week. She alternately played tough-kid parts, as when she slugged it out with another kid star with a tough image, Jackie Searl, in the 1935 film *Ginger*, and sweet roles, as in *The Farmer Takes a Wife*, made the same year. She kept working after Shirley Temple retired, but her film popularity began to wane as she grew into her teen years; it didn't help that the chubby little girl did not grow up to be anything but a plain Jane. She gave up the movies in 1947, got married, and moved to New Mexico.

Jane was back in Hollywood by 1956, but despite good roles in such movies as *Giant* (1956), she never regained her former stardom. Where Jane did hit it big, in the world that television had revolutionized, was in a series of commercials for a sink cleanser called Comet. She appeared in dozens of commercials in the 1960s and the early 1970s, playing Josephine the Plumber, who invariably wore overalls and who always solved someone's dirty-sink problem in the sixty-second limit set for a commercial drama. The cheerful, homely face that had made Jane Withers an appealing child star also helped to make her a convincing plumber. She gave up the Comet commercials after a few years, but she kept up her show-business contacts. In the mid-1970s Jane Withers was living comfortably in California and working to establish a Hollywood museum.

A more typical Hollywood story was that of Virginia
Weidler—more typical because she had good looks, played
good-child parts, and never really achieved acting success
after she grew up. The beginning of the story is familiar:
Virginia was born in California to stage-struck parents, who
escorted her and her six brothers and sisters through the
standard tour of the Hollywood studios. Virginia was the
one who caught on. At the age of four she made her debut
in a movie called *Surrender* (1931). However, she didn't
make the big breakthrough until the advanced age of seven,
when she played a brat called Europena in *Mrs. Wiggs of the
Cabbage Patch*, which starred W. C. Fields and Zasu Pitts.
Paramount signed her to a seven-year contract, and, although she never really scaled the heights, Virginia had
some good, meaty parts in such movies as *Girl of the Ozarks*
(1936) and *Souls at Sea* (1937).

Nevertheless, Paramount cut her loose after five years of
her contract. Virginia went over to MGM—she was all of
eleven at the time—and started a second career. You could
see her in one of the Andy Hardy movies, *Out West With
the Hardys* (1938); playing opposite an aging John Barrymore in a cynical comedy, *The Great Man Votes* (1939);
and doing some of her best work in a sparkling film version
of the Broadway play *The Philadelphia Story* (1940), in
which she played Katharine Hepburn's wasp-tongued little
sister.

Those were good years for Virginia Weidler. But the
movie business is tough—she learned that one day on the set
of *The Great Man Votes* when Barrymore, who thought she
was trying to steal a scene from him, literally threw her

Virginia Weidler is as grumpy as Roland Young and Cary Grant in this scene from *The Philadelphia Story*. (MGM, 1940)

across the room—and the fact that Virginia was getting older made things even tougher. When MGM picked up Shirley Temple in 1941, that was it for Virginia; the studio needed only one adolescent star. For all practical purposes, her film career was over. She made her last movie, *Best Foot Forward*, in 1943, flopped in a Broadway play, and settled down to marriage. More or less forgotten by the public, she died of a heart attack in 1968.

The sad truth is that for every Jane Withers who makes it big as an adult, there are a dozen Virginia Weidlers, who are quickly forgotten when they grow up. And not every child actor or actress makes it as big as Virginia Weidler did. Does anyone out there remember Peggy Lynch, who had something of a screen career in the 1930s and the 1940s? Peggy's original name was Robb. Her father changed her screen name because he didn't want to be overshadowed by his daughter, as had happened to Shirley Temple's father. He needn't have worried, because Peggy never really set the screen on fire. She played opposite Shirley Temple in a handful of films, was in a few "Our Gang" comedies, and had a few thrills in films with such as Bing Crosby (*The Star Maker*, 1939) and Greer Garson (*Blossoms in the Dust*, 1941).

Peggy's career continued into her teen years, but again she was never a headliner. Most typically, she was the double for the young Elizabeth Taylor in a movie called *National Velvet*. Wearing a black wig, Peggy stood in for Elizabeth in scenes that were regarded as too tiring for the star. There were more film roles and a new name, Margaret

Kerry, which was given to her in 1947. Peggy, or Margaret, continued acting teenagers into the television era. She gave up acting at the age of thirty-five and moved into a different career. All in all, it wasn't an unhappy story, although you can't find her name listed in some of the standard film reference books. At any rate, her story is a useful reminder for those who think that everyone in movies is a star.

But there are the exceptions, those who are truly stars. The kid-star boom continued into the 1940s, and one of the new stars to arrive on the screen was a girl named Margaret O'Brien. Reviewing one of her first films, a writer gushed, "Before we've completely forgotten about the natural charms and talents of Shirley Temple as the wonder-child of the movies, her place is being filled on the screen by another infant prodigy." That was written in 1944, when Margaret was only seven years old.

She was named Maxine when she was born in Los Angeles, and got her new name from her first big hit, *Journey for Margaret* (1942). She played a little British girl who was evacuated to the United States during the war, and she immediately captured the hearts of moviegoers. MGM knew a good thing when it came along, and Margaret was hard at work in no time. She made three films in 1943 and another five in 1944. In one of those movies, *Lost Angel*, she played a child prodigy who was being raised by a group of psychology professors and was introduced to the real world by a tough but tender newspaper reporter. "The tiny tot firmly establishes herself as the marvel of the current cinema," one reviewer wrote after seeing the film.

Margaret O'Brien does the cakewalk with her "big sister," Judy Garland, in *Meet Me in St. Louis.* (MGM, 1944)

And so she was. She could be funny with Red Skelton (*Thousands Cheer,* 1943) or Charles Laughton (*The Canterville Ghost,* 1944), be serious with Greer Garson (*Madame Curie,* 1943) and even hold her own alongside that masterful ham Orson Welles (*Jane Eyre,* 1944, in which she played a ballet-dancing French moppet). Many critics believe she did her best work as Judy Garland's kid sister in a classy film musical, *Meet Me in St. Louis* (1944). Dancing the cakewalk with Judy, giving a convincing portrayal of a child's fear at the possibility of having to leave her beloved home because her father had been offered a new job, Margaret did a memorable job. Partly because of her performance, *Meet Me in St. Louis* is regarded as one of the best film musicals ever made. She won an Academy Award for the part.

The Margaret O'Brien boom continued all through the 1940s, although the pace slowed down. She made only one film in 1945, playing alongside Edward G. Robinson in *Our Vines Have Tender Grapes,* and two in 1946, one of them a typical Wallace Beery Western called *Bad Bascomb.* But adolescence arrived, inevitably, and with that arrival Margaret's fame tailed off. The irresistible moppet was resistible as a teenager. She made a few films, appeared on stage, made some television appearances, married twice and gained a lot of weight. Very comfortable financially because of the money that was put away in a trust fund for her during her childhood, Margaret O'Brien today is a happily married mother who makes occasional acting appearances.

Just about everyone who went to the movies in those days remembers Margaret O'Brien. It takes a little more effort to recall another child star who was almost as big at the time, but who made fewer memorable movies and who faded out of sight faster—Gigi Perreau.

Gigi's real name was Ghislaine, and the way she broke into the movies is a Hollywood story of the kind they don't seem to make any more. Ghislaine Perreau was born in Los Angeles in 1941, because her parents were on the run from Hitler. Her father and mother had originally met in Japan and had gone back to France, their native country, when World War II broke out. When the Germans invaded, they were some of the lucky few who managed to get out. Gigi was born just three months after they arrived in the United States.

Her movie career started in equally dramatic fashion. Mrs. Perreau had ambitions for her son Gerald. She took him to MGM for a screen test one day, and had to take Gigi along because she had no baby sitter. Naturally, it happened that MGM was in desperate need of a cute little girl that day, because the moppet who was scheduled for the part had thrown a temper tantrum. Gigi was quickly thrust before the camera, looked good, and so made her movie debut at the age of two in *Madame Curie*, playing the famous scientist Marie Curie, as a child.

There were a couple of minor roles in the next few years, but Gigi didn't start rolling in high gear until she was seven years old. Samuel Goldwyn was looking for a boy and a girl to play, respectively, David Niven and Terèsa Wright as children for a movie called *Enchantment*. Once again,

Gerald went to try out for the part and Gigi tagged along. This time they both were hired. (Audiences didn't know they were brother and sister because Gerald used the stage name of Peter Miles.) Goldwyn liked Gigi enough to sign her to a seven-year contract—he was looking for a child star to match Margaret O'Brien—and before long she was not only making movies and stage appearances but was also earning an estimated $180,000 a year on commercial endorsements.

Like other child stars of that time, Gigi worked hard. She made three films in 1949, four in 1950, and three more in 1951. She appeared with Fred MacMurray in *Family Honeymoon* (1949), with Dana Andrews and Susan Hayward in *My Foolish Heart* (1950), and with Mark Stevens in *Reunion in Reno* (1951). In 1952 it was *Bonzo Goes to College*, featuring a trained chimp, and in 1953 it was . . . nothing. Just like that, Gigi's child stardom was over. Despite all the awards she had won, despite all the big money, she simply could not manage to retain her screen appeal when she stopped being a tot. That's show business.

Gigi didn't appear in a movie again until 1956, and then the parts were few and rather small. She and brother Gerald did make a television appearance or two (they had appeared together in half a dozen or more films), but the good old days were over. Gigi's last film appearance was in 1967, and she quickly drifted away from acting after that.

It was pretty much the same story with another girl star of the 1940s, Peggy Ann Garner. She was enormously effective in a 1943 film, *The Pied Piper*, in which bearded Monty

LONGFELLOW SCHOOL LIBRARY
BERKELEY, CALIFORNIA

Woolley played an Englishman who managed to get a gaggle of children out of France as the Germans marched in, and in *A Tree Grows in Brooklyn* (1944), a sentimental but not sticky story of growing up poor. But by 1949 she was playing in the likes of *Bomba, the Jungle Boy*, even though she had won a special Academy Award as an "outstanding child actress" in 1945. The unhappy truth is that outstanding child actresses can go out of date as fast as yesterday's newspaper.

CHAPTER 4

The Boys in the Bunch

If kid movie stars don't make it as adult movie stars, they usually can console themselves with comfortable trust funds, money that has been put aside for their later years out of their big childhood earnings. Those trust funds are there because of the unhappy experience of young Jackie Coogan, a kid who hit it about as big as anyone in Hollywood, and who learned that money sometimes can do strange things to people.

Jackie followed a familiar road to stardom. Born in 1914 to vaudeville parents, he made an appearance in an early silent film before the age of two and was on the vaudeville tour not long afterward. He was spotted by Charlie Chaplin, then one of the greatest stars in film, who was looking for an appealing young boy to star with him in a film called *The Kid*. The movie was about a tramp who picks up an abandoned child, learns to love him, and then gives him up for the child's own good. *The Kid* was released in 1921, and it was a smash hit. Both critics and audiences acclaimed not only Chaplin but also Coogan, the wistful waif who almost stole the film. At once, Jackie Coogan was a star.

He remained a star for years. In 1921 he was billed as "the greatest boy actor in the world," and in 1924 he was ranked with such as Mary Pickford and Rudolph Valentino. Films such as *Peck's Bad Boy* (1921), *Oliver Twist* (1921), and *Daddy* (1923) earned millions at the box office. Even though Jackie's charm faded slightly as he grew up, he could still get a contract from MGM for $1,300 a week when he was twenty.

But it wasn't his money. Just about all of it was going to his mother, who had married the family's business manager when Jackie's father died. Jackie had earned a total of nearly $4 million from acting. But when he came to claim some of that money, he was told that he had no legal right to it. He was even forced to leave the house that his money had earned. In his early twenties, Jackie Coogan found himself with no movie contract and no money. He got married (to a young starlet named Betty Grable) and filed suit for some of his earnings. After a long, bitter legal fight, he was awarded $126,000, but that didn't last him long.

If the suit didn't do Jackie much good, it did benefit many other child actors and actresses. Impressed by Jackie's sad experience, the California legislature passed what is formally titled the Child Actor's Bill, which everyone calls the Coogan Act. It says that at least fifty per cent of a child star's earnings must be set aside in a trust fund or some

Jackie Coogan in a publicity still for *The Kid*, the 1921 Charlie Chaplin movie that made him famous.

other form of savings. The act came too late to help Jackie, but it has helped many others.

Anyway, the Jackie Coogan story had a more or less happy outcome. He never regained his former stardom, but as the years went on he managed to make a more than comfortable living out of acting—not only occasional film roles but also television appearances, most notably as a chubby Uncle Fester in a monster series of the 1960s, "The Addams Family." And in 1972, when Charles Chaplin returned from a self-imposed exile in Switzerland (he had been driven out of the United States because of political controversy in the 1950s), there was a last emotional reunion.

The names are similar, but the story of Jackie Cooper is quite different from that of Jackie Coogan. The beginning is the same: stardom at an early age. Born in 1922, Jackie Cooper was raised in the middle of the California movie industry. His first film role came in 1929 in a musical, *Sunny Side Up*, made by the Fox studio, where his mother worked in the music department. That same year he began a stint with the "Our Gang" bunch. It ended in 1931, when he got the lead role in *Skippy*, a Paramount comedy based on a popular comic strip.

Jackie got an Academy Award nomination for *Skippy*, which made him a star. He stayed at the top for years, in a career that often had startling parallels to that of Jackie Coogan: In 1931 Cooper was starring with Wallace Beery in *The Champ*, a sudsy film about a boxer and a boy; in 1934 he starred in a remake of *Peck's Bad Boy*, which Coogan had made thirteen years earlier. He starred in *The Bowery*

That's Jackie Cooper on the right, with Jackie Searl on the left and Bobby Coogan (Jackie Coogan's brother), in *Skippy*. (Paramount, 1931)

with George Raft (1933) and *Treasure Island* with Beery again (1934).

But old age was approaching; Jackie was getting near adolescence. His career faded for a while in the late 1930s. The

LONGFELLOW SCHOOL LIBRARY
BERKELEY, CALIFORNIA

roles were mostly minor—one exception was a costarring
part with Henry Fonda in *The Return of Frank James*
(1940)—but Jackie kept working. He enlisted in the Navy
during World War II, made a couple of bad movies—with
Jackie Coogan, incidentally—when he was mustered out,
and then went to Broadway. Two stage successes restored
his reputation somewhat, and he returned to a Hollywood
where television had become big. Jackie mastered the new
medium very well, first in a situation comedy called "The
People's Choice," in which he played alongside a basset
hound named Cleo, and then in another comedy, "Hennessey," which ran for three seasons. Since "Hennessey" went
off the air, Cooper has been mostly a television executive, although he appears on television or in films now and then.
One sign of his talent was the Emmy he won for directing
one episode of "M°A°S°H." He started as a winner and has
kept it up ever since.

But Cooper did lose out once. He tried for the title role in
David Copperfield, a 1934 remake of the Dickens classic,
but the role went instead to a newcomer, twelve-year-old
Freddie Bartholomew. London-born Freddie was brought to
the United States by an aunt, who managed to get him an
audition before David O. Selznick, the movie's producer.
Freddie's English accent helped—Hollywood executives always seem to be entranced by the British—and he was off on
a sparkling career. Freddie played Greta Garbo's son in
Anna Karenina (1935), appeared with rough, tough Victor
McLaglen in *Professional Soldier* (1936), and was acclaimed in the title role of *Little Lord Fauntleroy* (which

Spencer Tracy sings a sea chanty to Freddie Bartholomew in
Captains Courageous. (MGM, 1937)

was taken seriously then but would be laughed off the stage today) that same year. Many think his best film role was opposite Spencer Tracy in *Captains Courageous* (1937).

That was just about the peak of his career. There were telltale signs of advancing age; after all, he was a ripe old thirteen. A 1938 movie, *Kidnapped,* an excellent film version of the Robert Louis Stevenson romance, saw him still at his peak, but the parts began to lessen after that. During the war he enlisted in the Air Corps. In the postwar years, his efforts to resume acting got him almost nowhere. His last film was *St. Benny the Dip* (1951). After that, he went into television, where he made an enormously successful second career in advertising.

If you wanted to be unkind, you could say that Freddie Bartholomew's British accent was a gimmick that helped him succeed in films. That would be unfair, because the accent was perfectly natural. Nevertheless, a gimmick can be a big help when you're just one aspiring youngster in a crowd of equally ambitious and equally attractive juvenile actors. And there has been no shortage of gimmicks in the movies.

Johnny Sheffield's gimmick appeared to be a loincloth, but it was actually his physical ability. Johnny made it big playing Boy, the son of Tarzan in the popular series of the late 1930s and 1940s. Those were the days when Johnny Weissmuller, a former Olympic swimming star, was playing Tarzan and Maureen O'Sullivan was playing Jane (Cheetah, the family chimp, played himself).

Johnny made his appearance in a movie called, naturally enough, *Tarzan Finds a Son* (1939). It wasn't easy money.

Although the actors never left Hollywood, even the back-lot jungle required a good deal of physical effort. Swinging from trees and dodging jungle animals, however tame, is hard work. But there were long breaks from the jungle routine. Johnny appeared with Mickey Rooney and Judy Garland in *Babes in Arms*, appeared with Pat O'Brien in *Knute Rockne—All-American* in 1940, and played opposite Priscilla Lane in *Million Dollar Baby* (1941) before stripping down to his loincloth again for *Tarzan's Secret Adventure* and a number of other sequels.

A funny thing happened to the Tarzan series. Everyone outgrew it. Maureen O'Sullivan was the first to go, dropping out for more serious roles in 1943. While the Tarzan films continued through and past the war years, both Weissmuller and Sheffield were growing—Sheffield up and Weissmuller sideways. At just about the time that Weissmuller got a bit too bulky to be Tarzan, Sheffield got too big to be playing a character called Boy.

Johnny Weissmuller put on the uniform of an African big-game hunter and became Jungle Jim in a series of standard, low-budget features that lasted until 1955. Johnny Sheffield, a strapping six feet tall and 190 pounds, stayed in his loincloth but became Bomba, the Jungle Boy. The first film, with that title, was made in 1949 and had Peggy Ann Garner as the female lead. The series went on for eleven more films until 1955, and featured such gems as *Bomba and the Elephant Stampede* and *Safari Drums*. It was killed by television, which also did away with Weissmuller's Jungle Jim series. Both series were intended for the bottom half of double features, in an era when Americans went to the movies for a whole evening's entertainment. When television came in, Americans got used to staying home. Double features died, and with them died Bomba, the Jungle Boy. Johnny Sheffield turned in his loincloth and enrolled in college. At last report, he was living happily in California, a sedate family man.

If Johnny Sheffield made a living out of a loincloth and a physique, young George Winslow made his fame on the bass of his voice. His nickname, "Foghorn," tells the story. From the time little George appeared on the then-popular television show "People Are Funny," his booming voice made him a public favorite. His television appearances led to his first movie role, in the 1952 film *Room for One More,* in which Cary Grant and his wife, Betsy Drake, played a softhearted couple who just couldn't resist adopting unwanted kids. George played opposite Grant in another 1952 film, *Monkey Business,* which also starred Marilyn Monroe; in between, he acted with Richard Widmark in a rather weepy movie about parental love called *My Pal Gus.*

Foghorn Winslow played opposite Marilyn Monroe again the next year in *Gentlemen Prefer Blondes,* a musical comedy in which he played a very young millionaire. The plot centered on the efforts of Marilyn and Jane Russell to marry money, and it was an amusing twist to have the little rich man say leering things to Marilyn in his surprisingly grown-up voice.

Alas, you know the rest of the story already. Little George was getting older, and his charm was starting to dim. He was a success in a 1953 movie with Clifton Webb, *Mister*

Scoutmaster, and picked up some money making television appearances, but he could not stop the relentless march of time. By 1958, when he was twelve years old, George "Foghorn" Winslow's movie career was over. He enlisted in the Navy and disappeared into the crowd.

With George Winslow it was a voice; with Butch Jenkins it was teeth and freckles. Butch looked just enough like the dream picture of the average American boy to make it in films: His buck teeth stuck out a mile, his freckles sprawled all over his face, and every mother and dad could identify with him. He was born in Los Angeles in 1937, and he was lucky on two counts. The first was pure location: If a Hollywood producer was looking for a child, why not look in the neighborhood of Hollywood? The second was parentage: Butch's mother was an actress, Doris Dudley. She had a rather minor role in a 1942 MGM movie, *The Moon and Sixpence.* Someone at the studio noticed Butch (his real name was Jack), and the next year he appeared in *The Human Comedy,* a warm story of Armenian family life in California, with Mickey Rooney and Edward G. Robinson, among others.

Everyone loved Butch, and the good roles came thick and fast. He appeared with Elizabeth Taylor in *National Velvet* in 1944, with Edward G. Robinson and Margaret O'Brien in *Our Vines Have Tender Grapes* in 1945, with Peter Lawford in *My Brother Talks to Horses* (a film whose title describes the plot) in 1946, and with Van Johnson and June Allyson in *The Bride Goes Wild* in 1948. And that was it. Being a movie star may sound like nothing but fun, but there was

Butch Jenkins paddles along with Margaret O'Brien in the flood scene from *Our Vines Have Tender Grapes*. (MGM, 1945)

pressure that got to Butch. He began to stutter, and nothing could stop him. His mother took him out of the movies. They moved to Texas, where Butch settled down to a normal life that has nothing to do with the movies. He is still doing quite well.

Sometimes, merely being in the right place at the right time can be the gimmick that leads to success. Brandon de Wilde, a child movie star of the 1950s, proved that point very well. He was born in 1942 in Brooklyn to a theatrical family, who never thought of an acting career for their son. But Brandon's father was the stage manager for a Broadway play, *The Member of the Wedding*, which had a role for a young boy. Someone suggested that Brandon might be good for the role, which was hard to cast, and he did get the part. The play opened early in 1950, ran for more than five hundred performances, and led to the same part in the 1952 movie version.

The next year Brandon de Wilde appeared in a movie that provided his greatest and most unforgettable role, the Western titled *Shane*, directed by George Stevens and starring Alan Ladd in the title role. Brandon played the son of a pioneering farmer family in the West, and Ladd played a gunman whose past was shrouded in mystery and who finally shot it out with the murderous Jack Palance, the gunman imported by the villain to drive the farmers off the range. The last scene, in which a wounded Ladd rides numbly into the distance, bleeding from wounds suffered in the gunfight, while Brandon shouts over and over, "Shane, come back!" is still memorable.

Brandon de Wilde never topped that role, although he did appear in some good movies in a brief career—most notably in *Hud*, in which Paul Newman played a western heel, in 1963. Brandon remained in the theater after he grew up. He was touring with the play *Butterflies Are Free* when he was killed in an auto accident in 1972, at the age of thirty.

Julie Harris, who had starred with him in *The Member of the Wedding*, concluded a tribute to Brandon by a quotation from another play: "I'll never forget you, Brandon. Never! Till the end of time."

Maybe it is unfair, but a lot of older moviegoers remember another child star of that time, Dean Stockwell, for just a few roles. One of them was the title role of a 1950 version of the Kipling story of India *Kim*. Another was the 1948 flop *The Boy with Green Hair*, a misbegotten sermon against discrimination ("Would you want your sister to marry someone with green hair?" one character in the film asked indignantly). Another was *Gentleman's Agreement*, a 1947 film whose message was that anti-Semitism is bad, for which Dean won a Golden Globe Award.

The trouble is that only old-time moviegoers are likely to remember Dean Stockwell. His story is, by this time, all too familiar: Born in California (in North Hollywood, to be precise) in 1936 to a theatrical family, spotted by a talent scout, a hit in his first big part, with Gene Kelly and Frank Sinatra in the 1945 MGM musical *Anchors Aweigh*. He was in a string of good roles in the next few years. Dean was an orphan befriended by a tough but gentle fighter, Wallace Beery, in *The Mighty McGurk* (1946), a country boy in *The Romance of Rosy Ridge* (1947), a cabin boy in *Down to the Sea in Ships* (1949), and an invalid who was nursed back to health by Margaret O'Brien in *The Secret Garden* (1951). But time was passing and Dean was growing; his last childhood role was in *Cattle Drive* (1951), when he was fifteen.

There have been adult film roles for Dean Stockwell since

Dean Stockwell and Lionel Barrymore in *Down to the Sea in Ships.* (Twentieth Century–Fox, 1949)

then, though none as good as those he had as a child. He has remained in the theatrical world, appearing in television features and movies, acting on the stage, and directing some plays. But those who want to recapture the old Dean Stockwell magic will have to go into the film archives to see those movies of the 1940s.

In the Dean Stockwell story and a lot of the tales of old (and not so old) Hollywood, you've noticed that growing up is not a happy experience for most child stars. As we'll see in a little while, not being allowed to grow up is an almost equally dismal fate that befalls some successful young actors and actresses. But before considering that brand of unhappiness, we can look at a relatively happy story, the story of the greatest kid show in the history not only of Hollywood but maybe of all show business—the "Our Gang" story.

CHAPTER 5

The Gang

Perhaps the best way to sum up the success of "Our Gang" is to say that Shirley Temple tried to join the team once and didn't make it.

Some explanations and qualifications are necessary. The time was the early 1930s, when Shirley was an unknown moppet. "Our Gang" was a roaring success and was besieged by literally hundreds of ambitious mothers and their aspiring children. Shirley never really got a chance to show what she could do. But after you give all those excuses, you come back to the fact that "Our Gang" could turn away the child who was to become Hollywood's greatest box-office draw and that "Our Gang" never suffered from it.

The Shirley Temple anecdote is just one incident in the life of "Our Gang." The complete story is much more impressive. Starting in the silent years, the series went on with-

out a break through the advent of sound and into the 1940s.
Along the way it had a number of different directors, and
several complete changes of cast as kids grew up and were
replaced. After more than two hundred episodes, the series
was killed; by then the original inspiration had failed. But
that death was just temporary. When television came along,
"Our Gang" was revived, with astonishing success. Under
the name "The Little Rascals," the old "Our Gang" series
lives on. It is peculiar to think that children today are still
laughing gleefully at movies that were made by kids who
have long since grown up, movies that were made in a
United States that was far different from today's hectic na-
tion, movies that were made with no thought of immortality
—but that might just go on delighting kids forever.

"Our Gang" was born in the fertile imagination of Hal
Roach, an American original. After drifting around the
world, Roach got into the movie business in the early years
of the century. By 1920 he had his own Hollywood studio
(actually in Culver City, near Hollywood) and was making
films by Harold Lloyd and other great film comedians.
Roach supposedly got the idea for a series that would feature kids after watching a bunch of ordinary kids playing
across the street from his office. His idea was that moviegoers would rather watch some plain kids who were up to
ordinary mischief than a bunch of artificial stage brats. He
was right.

The original "Our Gang" was recruited partly from the
ranks of child actors and actresses and partly from family
and friends of people around the studio. For the record, the
cast of the first film in the series, titled *Our Gang* and made

"Our Gang" in the 1920s. At the top, Farina Hoskins. Middle row, Mickey Daniels, Johnny Downs, Jackie Condon. Bottom row, Joe Cobb, Mary Kornman, Jay R. Smith.

LONGFELLOW SCHOOL LIBRARY
BERKELEY, CALIFORNIA

in 1922, consisted of Peggy Cartwright, Jackie Condon, Winston Doty, and Ernie Morrison, called "Sunshine Sammy." They were soon joined by Allen "Farina" Hoskins, Joe Cobb, Jackie Davis, Mickey Daniels, and Mary Kornman. Each child had something to contribute.

Ernie Morrison and Farina Hoskins were black children, who fortunately were not used in too much of the crude racial humor of that time. Joe Cobb became famous as the fat boy of the series. Mickey Daniels was tough but cute. The girls were real beauties, the kind that any parent (and any kid) could identify with. And the series was off and running.

From the start, the key to its success was reality. Hal Roach had wanted believable kids, and the studio had the sense to put those kids into fairly realistic situations. The many imitators who tried to follow the path of "Our Gang" almost always went wrong in the same way: They had exceedingly clever child actors and actresses doing exceedingly clever things, singing and dancing with great aplomb, and putting on thoroughly professional performances. But Hal Roach had discovered the great secret, a secret that has insured the success of "Our Gang" to this day: There is nothing quite as entrancing as the sight of perfectly ordinary kids getting into perfectly ordinary trouble. Any parent who has sat and watched his or her child do nothing in particular can testify to that. All Hal Roach and his directors had to do was to carry ordinary mischief just one step too far, and they had a great product.

Time passed. Joe Cobb grew up, and Roach started a nationwide contest to find another fat boy to replace him. The winner was Norman "Chubby" Chaney, who took over the role in 1928. Farina Hoskins grew up, and was replaced by Matthew Beard, Jr., whom everyone called "Stymie" and who was famous for his derby hat. Ernie Morrison bowed out after a couple of years. The cast kept changing, but the series always remained the same.

One amazing thing about "Our Gang" was the number of child actors and actresses who flowed through it at one time or another. Jackie Cooper was one of the future stars who first made his mark in "Our Gang," early in the 1930s. Dickie Moore was another. Scotty Beckett was a third.

After a couple of parts in other movies, Scotty joined the gang in 1934, when he was five years old. He stayed with the bunch for two years, appearing in fifteen episodes. In most of them, he was the kid in the baggy turtleneck sweater and cap who teamed with "Spanky" McFarland. Success with "Our Gang" brought Scotty offers for roles in Hollywood features, which is why his stay with the bunch didn't last longer.

One way to describe Scotty's screen roles is to say that he always seemed to be someone's son. He was Spencer Tracy's son in *Dante's Inferno*, a 1935 film about a rather unscrupulous adventurer who made his money in a carnival. He was Madeline Carroll's son in *The Case Against Mrs. Ames* (1936). For a change of pace, he was slaughtered by marauding tribesmen in India in a 1936 Errol Flynn swashbuckler, *The Charge of the Light Brigade*. Then he was the son of Greta Garbo (*Conquest*, 1937), of Wallace Beery (*The Bad Man of Brimstone*, 1938), of Norma Shearer and Tyrone Power (*Marie Antoinette*, 1938), and of Ralph

Bellamy (*Blind Alley*, 1939). Just to prove he didn't have to play someone's son all the time, in the 1941 film *Kings Row* he played a child who grew up to be Robert Cummings.

Even when he reached adolescence, an age that was disastrous for many young stars, Scotty Beckett continued almost without a break. He was the teenaged Al Jolson in the 1946 musical biography *The Jolson Story*. Without skipping a beat, he played William Bendix's son in a radio serial that was to become a TV show, "The Life of Riley." Everything seemed to be going well for him. He had an adult role as a young soldier in a fine film story of World War II (*Battleground*, 1949). But then began a long series of brushes with the law, when he was arrested for drunk driving. His career began to tail off. He was on television in a series called "Rocky Jones, Space Ranger," for a while in the mid-1950s, but the story was coming to an end. Scotty Beckett vanished from show business. He was found dead in his Hollywood home in 1968, at the age of thirty-eight. It was a tragic ending for a life that had begun so brightly.

In the saga of "Our Gang," Scotty Beckett's story is unusual both because he met such an unhappy fate but also because he left the gang for stardom in feature films. Generally, the "Our Gang" kids had a few years of episodes with the group and no nibbles from the big Hollywood world over the horizon before they gave up their film careers and went back to what can be called normal life. Most of the kids did try for other roles, and a few had some success, but "Our Gang" was just about the whole story for most of them.

Take two of the original gang, Mary Kornman and

Scotty Beckett as the young Al Jolson in *The Jolson Story*. (Columbia, 1946)

Mickey Daniels. Mary did tour in vaudeville after her original four-year tour with "Our Gang" (she came back now and again when she was older), and she did manage to get some parts in B films when she grew up. But she never made it really big, and eventually left show business for marriage. Mickey Daniels also did some film work after he left "Our Gang"—among other things, he appeared in another Hal Roach series, this one about teenagers, called "The Boy Friends"—but he never again hit the heights he had scaled as one of the Hal Roach bunch of kids. Eventually he went into the construction business.

Over the years, trivia fans have come to love "Our Gang." With the films still to be seen regularly on television, even middle-aged parents can get delight out of recalling which child star was in which episode of "Our Gang" and in trying to remember what became of each of their favorites. In the right circles, you can start a long, nostalgic conversation just by mentioning Spanky McFarland. A lad with a name as unforgettable as his looks, Spanky had plenty of opportunities to enlist nostalgia fans. He had one of the longest stays on record with "Our Gang"—eleven years, starting in 1932, when he was just a little more than three years old. Since he made so many "Our Gang" comedies, it's easy for many of his fans to forget that Spanky appeared in a number of feature films, but he did even while he worked with the gang.

Spanky was in a 1934 version of Robert Louis Stevenson's *Kidnapped;* in one of the first Technicolor films, *The Trail of The Lonesome Pine* (1936), which featured Fred MacMur-

Our Gang in the 1930s. At the center is Spanky McFarland, who autographed this picture for a friend.

Spanky McFarland

ray and Henry Fonda in a story about feuding country families and railroad builders; in a wartime movie, *Johnny Doughboy* (1943); and in not much else. Not too much of the money that he earned in the movies stuck with him after his show-business appeal vanished, but Spanky (call him George) eventually found a good job in business.

To a true "Our Gang" enthusiast, all you have to do is mention a name like Spanky to set off a torrent of memories. One such name is Darla (last name Hood), a pretty little girl who was with the gang for six years, starting in 1935. Darla had the luck to be discovered in the classic style. A Hall Roach scout spotted her in a New York hotel one night and arranged a screen test. The cute little dark-haired girl was in the center of the fun from then on. While she did get a few roles in some other Hal Roach films, Darla never made it big in feature films. But after her "Our Gang" career ended, she did quite well in the kind of show business that doesn't involve stardom—playing background music for films, making television and stage appearances, even doing voices for television commercials. Decades after her last "Our Gang" appearance, she still was recognized now and then by someone who had remained a fan of the series.

The reminiscences could go on and on. Many fans still recall "Buckwheat" Thomas (real name, William Henry Thomas), who lasted ten years with "Our Gang." One of the many black kids who were featured in the group, Buckwheat played a role more or less modeled after that of Farina Hoskins; even the names were designed to be similar. Off the screen, the two had remarkably similar careers after they grew up. Farina, who made more than a hundred "Our

Gang" shorts (more than anyone else), had a few movie roles later on, then dropped out of sight. He has spent most of his adult life helping others, working with the mentally retarded. Buckwheat quietly became a film technician when his "Our Gang" career ended. Neither of the two courted publicity.

All in all, the life stories of the "Our Gang" kids run the gamut from complete success to tragedy. Norman Chaney, the fat boy who succeeded Joe Cobb, died when he was just eighteen, in 1936. Tommy Bond, another "Our Gang" regular, went on to have a successful acting career in the 1940s. You can still see him now and then, when the Superman serials are revived, playing Jimmy Olsen, Clark Kent's young aide. Stymie Beard had a brief acting career, drifted into a tangle with drugs and emerged only years later, with the help of Synanon. Darwood Kaye, the bespectacled boy who appeared in "Our Gang" episodes in the mid-1930s, became a missionary. Porky Lee, who was active at about the same time, became a teacher. Shirley Jean Rickert, a beautiful little blonde, became a beautiful big blonde who worked in burlesque for a while before becoming a business executive.

All in all, literally dozens of kids appeared in "Our Gang" shorts over the years, some of them becoming regulars, many of them making only fleeting appearances. Not many of them became rich, because the salaries were not high. The biggest stars in the gang would earn perhaps three or four hundred dollars a week, and many of the lesser lights would get as little as forty dollars a week. All was not sweetness and light. With big money always over the horizon for those who could move on to starring roles in feature films, as Scotty Beckett, Jackie Cooper, and others did, there were inevitable rivalries and pressures. The surprising thing is how well the group held together, even as its makeup shifted consistently over the years, and how little trace there is on the screen of any kind of Hollywood phoniness.

"Our Gang" was able to survive so long, and to be revived in a new era and for a different medium, because the people in charge managed to let the natural high spirits of childhood shine through. Their competitors, kids series that included such talents as Shirley Temple and Mickey Rooney, occasionally flourished, but they have vanished almost without a trace. Talent wasn't the real secret of the "Our Gang" success. It was the skill with which Hal Roach selected the members of the group, and the ability of such directors as Robert McGowan, who handled many of the shorts, to make the chemistry work.

What killed "Our Gang" was not a shortage of ability but a change in the economic structure of the movie industry. Toward the end of the 1930s movie distributors began to place less emphasis on short subjects such as the "Our Gang" comedies. The distributors and the movie theaters they served wanted full-length features more than short subjects, at least short subjects of the length that just suited "Our Gang." The standard evening's entertainment was becoming the double feature—one "big" movie of top quality, one B film that served more or less as filler, and maybe a one-reel short, lasting about ten minutes, to usher people into and out of the theater.

The standard "Our Gang" products were two reels, or about twenty minutes long—too short to be features and too long to be fillers. Roach tried to adjust them both ways, making longer and shorter "Our Gang" episodes, but he wasn't happy with the results, either artistically or at the box office. In 1938 he sold the whole "Our Gang" operation to MGM, the great film factory of that era. MGM kept grinding out "Our Gang" shorts into the war years, making more than fifty one-reelers in all. Fans of "Our Gang" maintain that the MGM products were decidedly inferior to the Hal Roach episodes, even though some of the old (or young) regulars lingered on to the end.

In 1944 MGM made the last "Our Gang" episode, titled *Dancing Romeo*. In a real sense, however, the end never came. In the early 1950s, "Our Gang" shorts from the classic period were being revived in movie theaters. And after some hassles about copyrights and contracts, "Our Gang" comedies began to appear on television, labeled "The Little Rascals." (Interestingly enough, that was originally supposed to be the name of the group, but the title of their first short caught on as their name.) Television stations around the country are still showing old episodes over and over, although purists complain that too often crude cuts are made in order to fit in commercials.

The "Our Gang" television revival was good news for some retired regulars, who were invited to make appearances on TV shows. It was also good news for today's children, who can get a chance to watch these products of a Hollywood golden era. Talk about producing some new, modern "Our Gang" episodes has come to nothing. One problem seems to be a short supply of bright-eyed, innocent kids in this modern, television-wise world. At any rate, the old "Our Gang" is still around for our enjoyment.

CHAPTER 6

The Eternal Teenager

The pattern started with Mary Pickford, one of the very first stars to emerge in the movie industry. It has continued to this day on television. It is a pattern of eternal youth, comforting to the audience but frustrating for the actors who are caught in it. The audience can't stop tiny tots from growing up to be adolescents and adults, but it can stop teenagers from growing into adult life. Time and again the movie industry (and now television) has insisted that the stars it got to love as teenagers remain that way, despite the passage of time.

Mary Pickford was one of the first to find that out. She achieved stardom in the earliest days of movies, before the people who made films even realized that there could be such a phenomenon as a movie star. The first films to be made didn't even identify the actors and actresses in them.

Mary Pickford in *Pollyanna*. (United Artists, 1920)

LONGFELLOW SCHOOL LIBRARY
BERKELEY, CALIFORNIA

But moviegoers soon learned to pick out their favorites. One of them was "Our Mary," so called from a character she played (her real name was Gladys Marie Smith). She moved from a teenager career on the stage to making films with D. W. Griffith, the greatest of the early directors, as early as 1909. Her success in such films as *Tess of the Storm Country* (1914), *Rebecca of Sunnybrook Farm* (1917), and *Pollyanna* (1920) was phenomenal. Her greatest success was achieved with Adolph Zukor's Famous Players. By 1916 Mary was making $10,000 a week; by 1926 she was being paid $20,000 a week—and in an age when there was virtually no income tax and the dollar was worth many times more than it is today.

Behind those innocent eyes and beautiful curls was one of the shrewdest talents in Hollywood history. Mary Pickford was always good at getting the best financial deal for herself, and she was excellent in just about every area of filmmaking. She directed many of her biggest hits, and she had almost infallible judgment about her own material. The problem—if it was a problem—was that she could never grow up. She made *Pollyanna* when she was twenty-seven years old; the next year, in one of those things that can happen only in Hollywood, Mary played not only the title role in *Little Lord Fauntleroy*, in boy's dress, but also the role of the little lord's mother!

And moviegoers loved it. As far as they were concerned, Our Mary not only could but would have to stay young for the rest of her life. When she was thirty years old, for example, Mary Pickford asked her fans to suggest some roles they would like to see her in. Almost all the responses asked for teenage portrayals: Heidi, Alice in Wonderland, and so on. She sighed and went along.

Some very odd things happen because moviegoers want some favorites to remain young. It was in 1939, when she was sixteen, that Judy Garland was strapped into a corset that helped turn her into eleven-year-old Dorothy Gale of Kansas for *The Wizard of Oz*. One of the teenagers with whom Judy was attending school on the MGM lot was Lana Turner. Just about the time that Judy was turning back in age, Lana was being promoted as the "sweater girl," a sex goddess. Both Judy and Lana made Andy Hardy films, but Judy remained stuck in the teen years (as far as her screen image went) for a number of years, while Lana moved straight into seductive adult roles in such films as *Slightly Dangerous* and *Marriage Is a Private Affair*.

The same mysterious chemistry between audience and star still operates today. How else could you explain the transformation of a thirtyish actor named Henry Winkler into a television teenager called the Fonz? But it was different in the 1930s because movies were a mass-production industry, and there was a mad competition between the Hollywood studios to come up with teenage stars to match whoever the other film-makers had.

You may remember that a young singer named Deanna Durbin had an influence on the career of Judy Garland. It was an influence that affected a lot of other Hollywood teenagers, because Deanna's success was one of those amazing stories that no one could possibly believe as the plot of a movie—except that it really happened. Deanna not only skyrocketed from obscurity to stardom and from low pay to

Mischa Auer, Adolphe Menjou, and Deanna Durbin in *One Hundred Men and a Girl*. (Universal, 1937)

riches in a matter of months but she also saved an imperiled studio almost single-handedly.

Deanna was named Edna when she was born in Winnipeg, Canada, in 1921, but her life began changing within a year, when the family moved to California. She began taking singing lessons. In her early teens, she was seen by a talent scout, and was signed to a six-month MGM contract. But MGM let her go to Universal Studios in 1936 for the musical *Three Smart Girls*. It was a smash, and so was Deanna. Her next two films—*One Hundred Men and a Girl* (1937), which also featured conductor Leopold Stokowski and a symphony orchestra, and *Mad About Music* (1938)—also were colossal box-office hits. Universal, which had been a steady money-loser before Deanna came along, now was a big money-maker. So was Deanna; she went from next to nothing to $1,500 a week in less than a year. She was set in a formula as a wholesome teenager, as the titles of her movies indicate: *First Love* (1939), *It's a Date* (1940), *Nice Girl* (1941).

Deanna might have gone on playing teenagers forever, but she decided that it was time to grow up on the screen. It didn't work. Audiences didn't want to see a grown-up Deanna Durbin, and her box-office draw tailed off quickly. In 1949, quite comfortable financially, she retired from movies and went to live in France with her husband, film director Charles David. In the 1970s she was living in a small town near Paris, avoiding publicity and apparently quite happy.

Deanna Durbin's success meant that every studio had to have a wholesome teenage singing star. A hundred flowers bloomed, most of them briefly. It was no coincidence that Joe Pasternak, the Universal producer who had picked Deanna Durbin out of a crowd, came up with another winner, Gloria Jean. It was also no coincidence that both teenagers' careers tailed off badly after Pasternak left Universal;

it was Gloria Jean's bad luck that he left after working with her for only a couple of years.

Born in Buffalo in 1928, Gloria Jean dropped her last name, Schoonover, when she went into films. Her first film, *The Under-Pup* (1939), in which she played a poor girl who sang her way to popularity in a snooty summer camp for the rich, made her a star. In her next film, *If I Had My Way* (1940), she sang alongside no less a personality than Bing Crosby. It was another hit. Gloria Jean made only a few more films before Pasternak left Universal. One of them was the indescribable *Never Give a Sucker an Even Break* (1941), in which she played the niece of W. C. Fields. The script was written by Fields himself, and it made as little sense as anything that has ever been put on film. What with the great comic jumping out of airplanes, meeting gorillas face to face, being lowered by basket from a mountaintop retreat, and the like, Gloria Jean more or less got lost in the shuffle. Her career continued for a few years after that, but her popularity never hit the heights of her first films.

There was competition for more than singing talent in the Hollywood of that time. For example, if MGM had its teenage youth series, Andy Hardy, then Paramount had to have its teenage youth series, Henry Aldrich, which was based on a popular radio series (which, in turn, was based on a Broadway play). Hardly anyone except nostalgia buffs remembers Henry Aldrich these days, but the first films in the series show how much talent Hollywood had to throw around in its heyday. Henry was played by Jackie Cooper in the first film, *What a Life* (1939), and his sidekick, Dizzy, was played by Eddie Bracken. The screenplay had as impressive a pair of credits as could be imagined: Billy Wilder and Charles Brackett, one of the most successful teams in screen history. The same talent was available for the second Henry Aldrich film, *Life with Henry* (1941), but then the series settled down to a less spectacular course. Jimmy Lydon was cast as Henry and Charles Smith as Dizzy. There was the usual complement of supporting players: the stern father, the comforting mother, the frowning high school principal. The Henry Aldrich features were tailored for nothing more ambitious than the bottom half of double bills, and they did not take themselves seriously at all. Nevertheless, they were done with the practiced skill that was typical of Hollywood, and most of them managed to be amusing. Some say that the Henry Aldrich series stands up better than the Andy Hardy films, which had a lot more preaching in them about the virtues of home, flag, mother, and apple pie.

Andy Hardy tended to be taken somewhat seriously by MGM, while Henry Aldrich was regarded as nothing more than an amusing way to kill some time. The titles tell the story: *Henry Aldrich, Boy Scout; Henry Aldrich, Editor; Henry Aldrich's Little Secret; Henry Aldrich Haunts a House*. Henry always got into some silly, innocent trouble, blundered into one disaster or another, and somehow emerged not only unscathed but usually as a hero. Jimmy Lydon worked what could have been a tired formula with professionalism. Although he went on to a fairly successful run of film roles after the series ended, those who remember him still see him as Henry, the eternal teenager.

Probably the most outstanding case of arrested teenage

development in Hollywood history is that of the group which most people know as the Dead End Kids, although they appeared under many different names. For close to a quarter of a century this group of actors stayed frozen in time, somehow convincing their producers (if not their audiences) that they were reasonable imitations of teenagers.

The group got its start in 1936, when Sidney Kingsley's play *Dead End* was produced on Broadway. A stark drama about the bitterness of poverty in the Depression years, *Dead End* was filled with raw talk (at least for that era) and concluded with a shootout in which a gangster hero of the neighborhood boys was killed. Among the boys in the original cast were Huntz Hall and Charles Duncan. Later, Duncan was replaced by a young actor named Leo Gorcey. Gorcey and Hall, with other members of the Broadway cast, appeared in the film version of the play, which was released by Samuel Goldwyn in 1937.

Essentially the same group of actors remained together over the next few years, making such films as *Angels with Dirty Faces* (1938) with Jimmy Cagney, Humphrey Bogart and Ann Sheridan; *The Angels Wash Their Faces* (1939)—even then Hollywood had a penchant for sequels— and *They Made Me a Criminal* (1939) with John Garfield. By then, the pattern was set. The Dead End Kids were rough and tough on the surface but good at heart, always willing to be taught the honest way of doing things, and ready to help a pal in need. It was a pattern that lasted for many years.

The group broke up briefly in the late 1930s. Huntz Hall was at Universal, and Leo Gorcey was at Monogram Pic-

Leo Gorcey, left, and Huntz Hall, well on in years, play clowning teenagers in *Mr. Muggs Steps Out*, one of the "East Side Kids" features. (Monogram, 1945)

tures making "East Side Kids" features. They were reunited when Hall moved over to Monogram in 1946 to launch the "Bowery Boys" series. Leo Gorcey enlisted not only his brother David but also his father, Bernard. Others in the group included Bobby Jordan, Billy Benedict, and Gabriel

LONGFELLOW SCHOOL LIBRARY
BERKELEY, CALIFORNIA

Dell. Lasting about an hour, the "Bowery Boys" films were made to a rigid formula.

The leader of the group was Slip Mahoney, played by Leo Gorcey. A large part of Slip's efforts were devoted to fixing problems caused by his devoted but incredibly dense side-kick, Satch Jones, played by Huntz Hall. A plot twist that never seemed to get tired was to bestow some unusual talent on Satch: mind-reading powers, a great singing voice, re-markable strength. The boys were always having brushes with gangsters, or being sent off to some strange part of the world such as Africa or Paris, or running into ghosts or monsters. None of these details seemed to matter; neither did the poverty-row sets provided by Monogram, decidedly a budget-minded studio. And neither did the age of the "boys"; Leo Gorcey retired in 1955, when he was forty, but Huntz Hall kept going a few years after that. What killed the series was not the sight of potential grandparents playing teenagers but the decline of the double feature. Otherwise, the "Bowery Boys" might have gone on forever.

On some television stations they still are going on. Like "Our Gang," the "Bowery Boys" features had a revival when TV came along. An adult watching these films on television today may find them painfully unoriginal and crude, but kids still seem to like the slapstick and sheer high spirits of the Bowery Boys.

What is perhaps most impressive about the films today is their innocence. One would certainly expect that films about such upright, well-to-do youths as Henry Aldrich and Andy Hardy would avoid the seamy side of life. After all, the 1930s and the 1940s expected innocence from its teenagers. They were allowed a touch of puppy love, but no more than that; and they always hung out at the local soda fountain—nothing as strong as beer would ever cross the lips of Andy Hardy.

But the Bowery Boys were supposed to be tough slum kids who lived on the Lower East Side of New York, surrounded by tenements and gangland types. Nevertheless, the plot invariably had them hanging out in an ice cream shop run by a character named Louis Dumbrowsky, who was played by Bernard Gorcey. No stronger language than "golly" was to be heard from their lips. The air of total unreality that surrounded the whole enterprise didn't seem to matter. As long as the audience could watch Huntz Hall make faces at the camera and Leo Gorcey swat him over the head with his folded-up hat, they were satisfied. When Monogram gave up on the series, it was continued by Allied Artists. The last "Bowery Boys" film, *In the Money,* was made in 1958. Considering the quality of the material and the obvious aging of the cast, it was about time.

While the Bowery Boys, Henry Aldrich, and Andy Hardy all played good guys, there was also room in Hollywood for some teenage nastiness. One young lady who made a good part of her career playing nasty roles was Bonita Granville, whose future was shaped when she got the role of a malicious student who ruined the lives of two teachers by spreading rumors about them. The movie was *These Three* (1936), a film version of Lillian Hellman's Broadway play, *The Children's Hour,* and the teachers were played by Merle Oberon and Miriam Hopkins. Young Bonita won an Academy Award nomination for the role, and was immedi-

Bonita Granville gets Nazi punishment in *Hitler's Children*.
(RKO, 1943)

ately type-cast. She was a vicious witch-baiter in *Maid of Salem* (1937) and a spoiled rich girl in *Beloved Brat* (1938). Not all her parts were nasty though: She had a sympathetic role in *White Banners* (1938), which also starred Jackie Cooper, and played the lead in four Nancy Drew mysteries. She then appeared in *The Angels Wash Their Faces* with the Dead End Kids.

Hollywood had plenty of variety in those days. As time went by, you could see Bonita Granville as a cheerful visitor to Andy Hardy's home town, Carvel, in two films of that series, and getting whipped by the Nazis in a wartime film, *Hitler's Children* (1943). (Hollywood had some great shots at the Nazis, both before and during the war. One young actor, Skip Homeier, is memorable mostly for playing a vicious Hitler Youth who carried on his nasty totalitarian tactics after coming to the United States, but was reformed at the end in a 1944 film called *Tomorrow the World*.)

Bonita Granville never really grew up in the movies. Her attempts at adult roles were very successful. She made a good many television appearances in the 1950s, but it turned out that her real future was not in front of the camera. She had married John Wrather, a wealthy Texas oilman, and in 1950 he bought the popular TV show "Lassie." In 1964 Bonita Wrather (as she now prefers to be called) became the associate producer of the show. She became the producer a few years later and stayed in that position until "Lassie" went into syndication (which means they stopped making new episodes and sold the old ones for reruns) in 1972. When Lassie was revived for a 1978 movie, Mrs.

LONGFELLOW SCHOOL LIBRARY
BERKELEY, CALIFORNIA

Wrather was the coproducer. The former brat had made good in show business.

Amid the welter of teenagers who aren't allowed to grow up, it's interesting now and then to find one who isn't allowed to be young. Lana Turner was one. Jean Simmons, the British actress, was another. Even though she started in the movies when she was only fifteen, she hardly ever played a teenager. One exception was the film version of George Bernard Shaw's play *Caesar and Cleopatra* (1945), but it's an exception that doesn't matter, since she played a Cleopatra who was young in years but old in every other way. Another exception was the great film version of the Dickens novel *Great Expectations* (1946), in which Jean did play a young girl—but she appeared later in the film as the same character in her adult years. As we will see, that broke with a film habit of having one young actor or actress grow up to a different star later in the movie. Audiences just wanted Jean Simmons to be grown-up, and they got her that way.

The same rule still applies in contemporary television. It isn't so much the star's age, as the age that the viewer wants. Take the two Hardy Boys in the popular TV series. One of the two, Shaun Cassidy, is indeed a teenager, about the same age as the boy detective he portrays. But the other Hardy Boy, Parker Stevenson, was a Princeton graduate in his mid-twenties when he became a star playing the teenage sleuth. And John Travolta, the "Vinnie Barbarino" of the unruly Brooklyn bunch of students in the series "Welcome Back, Kotter," was also in his mid-twenties when he played a teenager not only on television but also in the hit movie

Saturday Night Fever. A teenage Travolta was what people wanted to see, and he dutifully played one both in a TV movie, *The Boy in the Glass Bubble* and in the film version of the Hollywood musical *Grease.*

Well, there are worse fates in acting—for example, the all-too-common disappearing act done by young stars when they start to get older. Given that alternative, many actors and actresses find that staying frozen in perpetual adolescence isn't that bad. Of course, the best fate of all is for a child star to become an adult star, and a few lucky ones have managed that.

CHAPTER 7

Growing Up to Be Someone

If you happen to catch an enjoyable 1949 musical called *In the Good Old Summertime* on television or in a revival theater sometime, stick around for the last scene. You'll see Van Johnson and Judy Garland, happily married according to the plot, strolling through the park, tugging a bewildered little girl between them. The infant, who looks more or less out of place, was Judy's real-life daughter; since the film called for only a brief nonspeaking appearance by a child, Judy's child was chosen for a lark.

Well, that little girl was Liza Minelli, who grew up to be as big a star as her mother had ever been, both on the stage and in movies. Liza's appearance in the movie is more a matter for trivia fans than proof that child actresses can grow up to be adult stars, but it is one way of making the point.

When we talk about child actors and actresses growing up to be somebody, we must distinguish carefully between growing up in real life and growing up on the screen. As we have seen, it is standard Hollywood practice to have a character in a film played first by a young actor or actress and then by an adult. That practice can lead to some startling metamorphoses, such as Mickey Rooney growing up to be Spencer Tracy: Rooney played the title role in *Young Tom Edison*, and Tracy starred in the sequel, *Edison the Man*. The way the films work, almost any kid can grow up to be almost any adult. Mickey Rooney also grew up to be Clark Gable in *Manhattan Melodrama* (1934). Freddie Bartholomew grew up to be Tyrone Power in *Lloyds of London* (1936). In a single year, 1945, young Darryl Hickman grew up to be both Robert Alda (in *Rhapsody in Blue,* a film biography of George Gershwin) and Fred MacMurray (in *Captain Eddie,* a biography of aviator Eddie Rickenbacker).

The list could go on and on. In *Kings Row* (1942) Scotty Beckett grew up to be Robert Cummings. A few years later he grew up to be Larry Parks, who was playing Al Jolson in *The Jolson Story* (1946). In *Cavalcade*, a movie that won the Academy Award in 1933 but is almost forgotten today, one of the few Americans in an almost all-British cast, Bonita Granville, grew up to be Ursula Jeans. Young Terry Kilburn grew up to be the British actor John Mills in the classic *Goodbye, Mr. Chips* (1939). (Just to confuse the issue, the plot had Terry playing four generations of boys from the same family in the saga of a beloved British teacher.) And we've noted that Jean Simmons remarkably grew up to be herself in *Great Expectations,* playing the charming but icy Estella both as a young girl and as an adult.

"Growing up" to be an adult actor or actress in a movie is easy. But growing up in real life to become an adult star is not at all easy for most child actors and actresses. Indeed, none of the movie transformations mentioned here is as amazing as the way in which a child actor named Mickey Gubitosi grew up to be first a psychotic killer (on film) and then a rough-and-tough television detective named Baretta. That metamorphosis puts the Liza Minelli story in the shade.

Born in 1933 to a working-class family in Nutley, New Jersey, Mickey was pushed into a stage career by his parents by the time he was two years old. The family moved to California, where Mickey caught on as a member of "Our Gang" in the declining MGM years of that series.

When that assignment ended, Mickey moved on to playing the improbable role of Little Beaver, the young Indian sidekick of Red Ryder, a B-movie Western hero in a series that got its start as a comic strip. It was highly forgettable work; the cheap Westerns that were turned out by the gross in double-feature days vanished without a trace when the double bill went out of style. By then Mickey Gubitosi had become Robert Blake, and he picked up a few good roles as he toiled on through his childhood years. Those who love trivia never forget that Robert Blake is the little Mexican boy who sells Humphrey Bogart a winning lottery ticket in the 1948 classic of greed and gold *The Treasure of the Sierra Madre.*

That's young Robert Blake as Little Beaver with Don "Red" Barry in the Red Ryder series. (Republic, 1944)

Then came adolescence, and troubles. Expelled from several schools, Blake went heavily into drugs. A new age of frankness had begun, and Blake soon was telling interviewers that he had never been happy as a child and that he indulged in both crime and narcotics during his teen years. In days gone by, that confession would have been enough to end an acting career. But the new climate in Hollywood helped Blake, especially because his talent was obvious. In his twenties he began picking up roles in some minor films and on some televisions shows. His natural toughness kept him back, because Blake had a habit of refusing to compromise; he was literally willing to fight anyone who didn't want to do things his way.

Even his first big adult breakthrough, as a merciless killer in *In Cold Blood* (1967), boomeranged on him. Blake became so emotionally involved in the task of portraying the character he played that his career suffered for several years. When he got back on the track, he had some good parts—the title role in a Western about an independent-minded Indian, *Tell Them Willie Boy is Here* (1969), and a cop in *Electric Glide in Blue* (1973)—but the trouble was that none of his films were big box-office successes. He missed out on some really big roles, such as the lead in *Lenny* (Dustin Hoffman got the part) and the role of Billy Rose in *Funny Lady*—supposedly because he insulted Barbra Streisand when she wanted him to audition for the part.

Then came "Baretta," the television series in which Blake cleaned up as a cockatoo-carrying, street-wise detective. His success on TV has been so great that most people have forgotten Robert Blake (or Mickey Gubitosi), the child actor.

Since Blake is as tough as ever, future chapters in his life story promise to be at least as interesting as his past.

The Robert Blake story is typical in one respect: Fame as an adult star can easily blot out any memory of a childhood career. The prime example of that is Elizabeth Taylor. How many people today remember that this highly publicized, often-married sex goddess made her first appearance on the Hollywood scene as a little slip of a girl with a shy, winning manner and a captivating British accent?

Up to a point, the Elizabeth Taylor story is right in line with that of your average child actress. Born in England in 1932, young Elizabeth came to the United States with her parents because of World War II. After a couple of minor roles (one of them with Alfalfa Switzer in a short, *Man or Mouse*), she first made her mark in the 1943 movie that got the Lassie series started, *Lassie Come Home*. The next year, she died a plaintive death as the friend of the heroine in *Jane Eyre*. The same year, she grew up to be June Lockhart in a romance about England in World War I, *White Cliffs of Dover*. But her really big childhood hit was in the role of a horse-loving British girl who rode her horse to victory in the big race in *National Velvet* (1944), a movie that also starred Mickey Rooney.

Adolescence was rapidly approaching. But Elizabeth made two transitions without much effort at all. The first was from a winning young girl to a charming teenager, in such films as *Courage of Lassie* (1946), *A Date with Judy* (1948), and *Little Women* (1949). Almost immediately, she became a starlet as the young bride in two family comedies,

Mickey Rooney and Elizabeth Taylor in the horse-racing film *National Velvet*. The horse is in the background. (MGM, 1944)

Father of the Bride (1950) and its sequel, *Father's Little Dividend* (1951), both with Spencer Tracy and Joan Bennett. And right after that she became a genuine star, recognized as one of Hollywood's great beauties, playing the spoiled rich girl in *A Place in the Sun* (1951), a film in which Montgomery Clift committed murder for the love of her.

The rest of the story is familiar to anyone who reads fan magazines and headlines: a number of marriages, a long string of appearances in movies both forgettable (such as *Love Is Better Than Ever* and *Rhapsody*) and memorable (such as *Cleopatra*), with lukewarm reviews from the critics but constantly increasing paychecks. At this stage of the game, Elizabeth Taylor is not so much an actress as a star, someone people come to see not because they expect to see great acting but because she is Elizabeth Taylor. And somewhere in the distant past is that youngster who made good playing little-girl roles in what now seems to have been Hollywood's age of innocence.

Someone who followed the same path as Elizabeth Taylor, but hardly with the same spectacular flourishes, is Natalie Wood. Once again, a lot of people have trouble remembering that the woman who played the burlesque stripteaser Gypsy Rose Lee in the 1962 musical *Gypsy* got her start in movies as a little girl. But Natalie did make her first film appearance when she was just five years old, in the 1943 film *Happy Land*. The movie was made on location in her home town, Santa Rosa, California, and she was recruited along with some other children to appear as an extra. She did well enough to get a credit line—under her original name, Natasha Gurdin—and to be called by the director three years later to appear with Orson Welles and Claudette Colbert in a three-handkerchief movie called *Tomorrow Is Forever*.

That got Natalie really started in movies. In 1947 she made a big hit in a movie that still shows up on television every Christmas, *Miracle on 34th Street;* she played a cynical little girl who started off being very skeptical about the existence of Santa Claus but ended up as a sentimental believer. In that film she was Maureen O'Hara's daughter. The same year, she was Gene Tierney's daughter in a charming tale of the supernatural, *The Ghost and Mrs. Muir,* with Rex Harrison playing the ghost.

Instead of growing up to be someone, Natalie's film pattern was to be someone's daughter: Walter Brennan's daughter in a 1949 movie, *The Green Promise;* Fred Mac-Murray's daughter in *Father Was a Fullback;* Joan Blondell's daughter in *The Blue Veil* (1951); and even Bette Davis's daughter in *The Star* (1953).

At that point Natalie's career took a brief pause. But she was back in films in a big way when she was cast opposite James Dean and Sal Mineo in the 1955 film about the troubles of American teenagers *Rebel Without a Cause.* The film showed she had that elusive something called star quality, and the good parts began coming her way: with Gene Kelly in *Marjorie Morningstar* (1958), with Warren Beatty in *Splendor in the Grass* (1961), and especially in two big musicals, *West Side Story* (1961) and *Gypsy* (1962). But in the late 1960s, after some less than impressive movies, her career began to fade. Natalie made a big comeback in a 1969 comedy, *Bob & Carol & Ted & Alice,* earned a lot of money because she had a share in the profits, and has more or less been out of acting ever since.

Changing from child star to adult star is one thing; changing from child star to adult ape star is another. Rather un-

Natalie Wood is comforted by Edmund Gwenn, who is trying to convince her that he is Santa Claus in *Miracle on 34th Street*. (Twentieth Century–Fox, 1947)

fairly for an actor who has been excellent in many different roles, Roddy McDowall is known to many film fans as the boy who started out by being Lassie's friend and went on to become the mask-wearing hero of the seemingly endless "Planet of the Apes" series of science fiction films.

Roddy was born in London in 1928, began acting in British films by the age of eight, and had appeared in more than thirty movies, usually in minor roles, when he and his mother were evacuated to the United States in 1940. He was an enormous hit in *How Green Was My Valley,* Darryl F. Zanuck's 1941 production about a Welsh mining town, in which Roddy played a sensitive boy who had to become a coal miner. Roddy did his share of growing up to be someone else over the following years. He grew up to be Tyrone Power in *Son of Fury* (1942), Gregory Peck in *The Keys of the Kingdom,* a 1945 film about a priest in China, and Peter Lawford in another 1945 film, *The White Cliffs of Dover.*

But, curiously enough for someone who was to grow up in real life to play a bizarre animal role, Roddy did some of his most memorable work in movies as a young friend of animals. *My Friend Flicka* (1943) cast him as an American boy who loved a rebellious horse. Audiences accepted Roddy in the role of a son of a western family despite his accent, and the film led to a sequel, *Thunderhead, Son of Flicka.* Meanwhile, moviegoers were also seeing Roddy as a British boy in love with a dog who managed to find its way home even though it was sold and taken far away. *Lassie Come Home* (1943) started a long series that went on well into the television years.

In 1945, when Roddy was moving into what looked like

The film is *Lassie Come Home,* and the stars are Elsa Lanchester, Roddy McDowell, Lassie, and Donald Crisp. (MGM, 1943).

his awkward teenage years, his contract with MGM came to an end. For a while, so did his film appearances, at least for a couple of years. Roddy got back into the movies by acting both on stage and on television, proving that the boy actor

LONGFELLOW SCHOOL LIBRARY
BERKELEY, CALIFORNIA

had become an adult actor. In the 1960s he had good parts
in such films as *Cleopatra* (1962) and *The Greatest Story
Ever Told* (1965). He also became part of the Walt Disney
stock company, appearing in several of Disney's family-
oriented comedies—*That Darn Cat* (1965) with Hayley
Mills and *Bedknobs and Broomsticks* (1971) with Angela
Lansbury, among others.

Then came the apes. The first of the series was *Planet of
the Apes* (1968), which starred Charlton Heston as an
American astronaut marooned on a planet where chimpan-
zees and gorillas ruled and humans were hunted and de-
spised. The film went over so well at the box office that a
string of four sequels followed. Roddy MacDowall was in
four of the pictures, speaking his lines through an ape's face
mask and playing Cornelius, who eventually became the
hero of the series. For a while it appeared that Roddy would
never get the mask off. Television started a "Planet of the
Apes" series, and Roddy got a leading role. For better or
worse, the series flopped, and Roddy went back to playing
human beings—which he still does quite well.

The latter part of the Roddy MacDowall saga is one indication that things were changing for child stars. Television
had arrived, which meant not only that Hollywood was
making fewer movies but also that a whole new kind of
show-business career had opened up. Some things remained
the same, though, as the story of Sally Field indicates.

Sally became famous as the heroine of the television series
"Gidget," in which she played a 1960s version of the familiar
typical American teenager, the kind that used to show up in

Andy Hardy or Henry Aldrich movies. From there, she moved on to the starring role in "The Flying Nun," a series about a teenage novice who would take to the air when the plot called for it. In the old Hollywood days that sort of nonsense was accepted as part of the game. In the new, serious atmosphere of the 1960s and 1970s, it turned out to be no fun at all. In her mid-twenties, Sally Field dropped out of sight for a year or two. Typically, she went to the Actors Studio to study her trade.

When she reappeared, it was in some deadly serious roles. One of them was in the television movie *Sybil,* in which she played a mentally disturbed woman with sixteen different personalities. In 1977 she appeared with Henry Winkler in *Heroes;* he was a Vietnam veteran and she was a mixed-up woman who got straightened out by helping him. On the lighter side, she appeared with Burt Reynolds in *Smokey and the Bandit,* a comedy that featured cars as much as it did people and that was a surprise hit. It was only then that Sally felt she had lived down the jokes about the Flying Nun and could go ahead with a serious adult career.

The story of Hayley Mills was an even more interesting sign of the way things were changing. Hayley got into the movies because her father, the British star John Mills, was up for a role as a detective pursuing a fugitive in the 1959 movie *Tiger Bay.* The film was supposed to star a young boy, but that was changed to make it a girl's role after the producer saw Hayley. Walt Disney saw *Tiger Bay* and signed Hayley to a long-term contract. Sweetness and light was the word at the Disney studio: Hayley played the lead

Hayley Mills tangles with Dean Jones in *That Darn Cat* (Buena Vista, 1965)

in a new version of *Pollyanna* (1960), in a Jules Verne swashbuckler called *In Search of the Castaways* (1962), in *The Moonspinners* (1964), and in *That Darn Cat* (1965).

But she was also offered the role of a sexy young teenager in *Lolita*, a part she turned down. And by 1967 she was acting in a British comedy-drama called *The Family Way*, which had her playing a young married woman and which centered on sex. In the old Hollywood, a child actress's first kiss was a tremendous thing. In the new Hollywood, kissing wasn't such a big deal. The old innocence was disappearing rapidly, and a new kind of child star was arriving on the scene.

CHAPTER 8

Modern Times

In 1978 Franco Zeffirelli was holding an audition to select a boy to play in the latest version of the old story *The Champ*. The boy who won the part, in the full light of all the publicity that Zeffirelli could muster, was a seven-year-old from Staten Island named Ricky Schroder. Although he was only in the second grade at the time, Ricky was rather composed as he told reporters that this sort of thing wasn't a novelty to him. He'd been on camera since the age of three months, when he starred in a diaper commercial. In between that bare-bottomed appearance and *The Champ* was a long string of other television commercials and modeling appearances. In short, Ricky made it clear that he is a child of the TV age.

One of the features of that age, at least for show business, is that child actors don't have to get their start by toddling

LONGFELLOW SCHOOL LIBRARY
BERKELEY, CALIFORNIA

out on a stage or being pushed into a movie screen test by an ambitious mother. The advertising industry now provides an even better door to acting. Hundreds or thousands of commercials are made every year, and an almost endless supply of good-looking children is needed. Instead of being able to weep on cue in a tearful movie about widowhood, today's aspiring young actor or actress must be able to whip up instant enthusiasm about a breakfast food or a dog food or a frozen pizza or whatever else is being sold over the airwaves. Success in commercials can easily lead to an acting career.

Or it can just lead to more success in commercials, which can be an acting career in itself. Since a single commercial can bring an actor or actress tens of thousands of dollars if it is shown often enough, a lot of kids who are hits in commercials just don't move on to anything else. It's kind of like the Hollywood in which some kids remained part of "Our Gang" forever (or at least until age caught up with them), but somehow it feels different.

Sometimes just one commercial is enough. In 1971 a three-year-old New York boy named John Gilchrist made a commercial for a cereal called Life with his two older brothers, Thomas and Michael. In the commercial, the two older kids tried out the cereal on their brother "Mikey" and exclaimed, "He likes it!" The commercial was a big hit, and the ad people quickly turned out a sequel that was still being shown on television seven years later. In addition, John Gilchrist got his picture on the box of Life cereal. The money came rolling in over the years, but young John didn't do much more in the way of commercials later. Someone occasionally asks him for an autograph, which he gives, but aside from that he's pretty much an ordinary boy—except that he has a lot of money from that commercial in the bank.

It's quite a different story for Mason Reese, who was the reigning king of pint-sized commercial superkids in the 1970s. Blessed with an unusual voice and a chubby, owlish face, Mason first hit it big in 1973, when he was six years old, with a commercial for an Underwood meat product. Soon he was making appearances as a cohost on the Mike Douglas talk show, working as a reporter—the youngest in the history of television—on a New York City radio station, and being called a "media brat" by *People* magazine. And, of course, he made commercials—for Dunkin' Donuts, Birds Eye, and a host of others. Mason kept trying to move into a television series or do some other kind of serious acting, but commercials seemed to be what people wanted him to do.

The commercials business is just one of the new features of the television age. Another novelty is that television gives almost every child a chance to be a star, at least for a day. Many television stations have shows that feature neighborhood kids, either playing games or competing for prizes, with a new batch of kids brought in periodically. "Romper Room," which featured preschool children (and which was criticized for having such a hard sell for its toys, was the most prominent of these shows, but most cities have had comparable programs on local stations. In New York, for example, a show called "Wonderama" flourished for a decade before it folded in the mid-1970s. It was a Sunday morning show that allowed kids to compete in funny contests (like

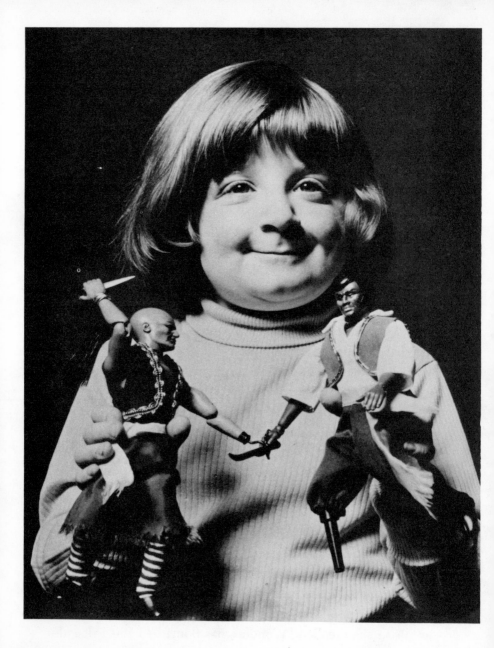

Mason Reese, the king of the commericials in the 1970s.

bat-the-balloon) and that brought in a miscellaneous collection of vaudeville acts and personalities to fill the time. In its heyday, "Wonderama" had a waiting list several years long; kids who were signed up when they were three years old got on the show when they were six or seven.

Television has another remarkable quality: It allows viewers literally to grow up with child stars, and it has tagged some of those stars indelibly with their television roles. In the movies, it seemed that kids didn't have to grow up so fast. You saw a movie star only once or twice a year, in most cases, so it was easy to overlook the growing the star did between appearances. On television, you see the actor or actress every week. In addition, there are reruns of the episodes to remind you of what the star looked like a few months ago. A movie series like "Our Gang" could go on almost forever as new characters replaced the kids who had grown up. But television series which star kids must come to an end sooner or later, because the kids outgrow their parts.

So it was with one of the biggest hits in television history, a series called "Father Knows Best." The show, which began a seven-year run in 1954, had Robert Young as the father and Jane Wyatt as the mother. Their three television children were played by Lauren Chapin (who was Kathy), Elinor Donahue (who was Betty), and Billy Gray (who was Bud). The show was unusual because it treated its characters as real people. As one television critic noted, *Father Knows Best never has introduced into the script an unexpected millionaire uncle from New Zealand nor a housemaid who is actually a Bavarian baroness incognito. The chief ap-*

peal of the program lies in its close relationship to events that occur regularly among families all over the country."

That was fine for a while. But eventually, the Anderson family (as it was named) grew up. Bud would have to go away to college, and Betty would have to get married. Rather than get into those complications, the show was folded. But it is typical of television that some stations are still showing reruns of the original episodes. Occasionally a rerun of "Father Knows Best" bumps up against a rerun of "Marcus Welby, M.D.," in which Robert Young played a doctor a few years later.

Occasionally the television audience has a chance to watch a child grow up over many years and through many different shows. Young Ronny Howard made his first television appearance in the black-and-white days of 1956, on an episode of "Kraft Theatre," when he was just two years old. He had some appearances off the tube, including a role in the movie musical *The Music Man* (1962), with Robert Preston, but Ronny made his big impact on television. He played Andy Griffith's son in "The Andy Griffith Show," which had an eight-year run in the 1960s and is still being shown in reruns, and also made a number of appearances on other television shows. When he grew up, Ron Howard made a successful acting transition to play Richie Cunningham with Henry (the Fonz) Winkler on "Happy Days," an unrealistic but popular 1970s version of teenage life in the 1950s. Ron was in his mid-twenties by then, and he was showing some dangerous signs of becoming a permanent teenager; one of his big movie successes was as a teenager in *American Graffiti*, a 1975 recollection of what life had been like for California teenagers in the 1950s.

Television shows have to keep making continual adjustments as their child stars grow visibly older year to year. One of the big hits of the late 1950s and early 1960s was a show called "Leave It to Beaver," which starred an attractive boy named Jerry Mathers as "Beaver" Cleaver, the youngest child in a typical American family. When the show started, Jerry was a tyke of six, with a hint of a lisp and little-boy qualities. When "Leave It to Beaver" went off the air in the 1960s, the script writers were wondering whether they should allow Beaver to smoke a pipe, and they had allowed him his first screen kiss. Just to show how the world has changed since then, a rumor that Jerry Mathers was killed in Vietnam was widespread in the 1970s among the adults who had grown up watching his show. In fact, Jerry Mathers was an insurance salesman in California in 1978.

At the same time, a sailor named Jay North was serving on the U.S.S. *Iwo Jima,* an aircraft carrier. Jay became famous by playing Dennis the Menace on television from 1959 to 1963. He started playing the comic-strip role when he was seven years old—he had been acting for a few years before that, mostly in commercials—and outgrew it within a matter of years. Some kids, like Mason Reese, seem to stand still (Mason, at the age of eleven, was complaining because he was only fifty inches high). Jay North grew like a weed—more than six inches in two and a half years. It was Jay's bad luck to lose his cuteness as he grew up. After a while audiences simply would not accept him as a pint-sized terror whose special target was the irascible neighbor Mr. Wilson. Jay North appeared in a couple of movies after his stint as Dennis the Menace ended, and had a brief run in a TV series titled "Maya," but his show-business career hit a dead

LONGFELLOW SCHOOL LIBRARY
BERKELEY, CALIFORNIA

Jay North as *Dennis the Menace*.

end by the time he was a teenager. He enlisted in the Navy when he was twenty-five, and survived a lot of kidding about his television career by his shipmates.

Another television kid who outgrew the part was Tommy Rettig, who played Lassie's pal, Jeff Miller, for four years starting in 1954. Tommy was eleven years old when the series began, and by the time he got to be fifteen, he was no longer acceptable as a kid star. It was a bitter blow for a boy who had shared in an Emmy won by the show and who could tell about having dates with Marilyn Monroe. The producers of the show managed the changeover with typical ingenuity. The plot had Jeff Miller's family leaving the country, and giving their dog to a forest ranger and his young sidekick, played by eleven-year-old Jan Provost. Tommy Rettig tried to make it as a teenage actor but didn't succeed. In one of the unhappier endings in show-business stories, he was found guilty of a drug charge in 1976 and was sentenced to prison.

Tommy Rettig complained that his stint as Jeff Miller had type-cast him so that he couldn't get other roles. That seems to be a constant complaint. Jay North said that directors always saw him as Dennis the Menace. A teenager named Dwayne Hickman, who played the lead role in a foolish TV series, "The Many Loves of Dobie Gillis," never really played anyone else after that. Jerry Mathers was Beaver Cleaver, and that was about it. Of course, the phenomenon of having your career cut short by old age is nothing new for child stars; it happened over and over again in the golden age of Hollywood. What is new these days is that some child stars' careers are limited to playing one role on a television series; by the time the series ends, they've outgrown their charm.

Something new that has also arrived in the television era is nastiness (for want of a better word). Bluntly, the kids aren't what they used to be, either on television or in the movies. In the old days, Bonita Granville could create a sensation by playing a vindictive child; her role was a sharp contrast to that of the typical child star, who said things like "Jeepers" and guzzled malted milk. Nowadays you never can tell what sort of bad stuff a kid is likely to generate.

You could see it coming when Patty McCormack made a hit as a young monster in a movie called *The Bad Seed* (1956). As a child actress, Patty had a sort of normal beginning. She was discovered at the age of four in a New York restaurant: Her mother had taken her on a shopping tour because no baby sitter was available, the restaurant where they were having lunch staged a modeling contest, and Patty won. That started her on a modeling career, which led to the starring role in a Broadway show, *The Bad Seed*. Patty played a little girl who was born vicious and who murdered three people in the course of the action. It went over so big that Patty got the role in the film, and won an Academy Award nomination for her portrayal of viciousness. The audiences who once wanted not much else but sweetness and light now were ready to applaud a child star who was rotten to the core.

But in real life Patty was anything but rotten. The daughter of a Brooklyn fireman named Frank Russo (her stage name came from her grandmother), Patty managed the difficult job of being a star and a good kid simultaneously.

Patty McCormack in a scene from her television series "Peck's Bad Girl."

She had a parochial school education, cheerfully played good-kid parts as well as monsters (she was one of the family in "I Remember Mama," a warm-hearted television series about a Scandinavian family), played a few movie and television roles as a teenager, and then went on to live a normal life as an adult.

Patty Duke as the lovable American teenager, 1960s style, in her television series "The Patty Duke Show."

Along the way, Patty won an Emmy for playing the young Helen Keller in the television version of the drama *The Miracle Worker*. The play was a vigorous rendition of the story of Helen Keller, a girl who was born deaf and blind and who was educated by the efforts of a devoted teacher, Anne Sullivan. It depicted that education as a series of violent physical bouts—throwing chairs, banging tables, pushing and shoving, as Anne Sullivan tried to get through to her young ward.

In the movie version of *The Miracle Worker* (1962), as in the original Broadway production, Anne Sullivan was played by Anne Bancroft and Helen Keller was played by another Patty, a youngster named Patty Duke. The violence was filmed so realistically that both the stars had to wear pounds of padding under their clothes; Patty even wore a catcher's chest guard. She won an Academy Award for the portrayal, and moved on to even bigger television success in "The Patty Duke Show." In that series Patty played both an American girl and her visiting British cousin.

On the screen she was lovable. Off the screen she was a terror. She gained a reputation for throwing tantrums, and it was impossible to predict what she would say in public. Even though her acting seemed to be as good as ever (she won an Emmy for her role in a television drama, *My Sweet Charlie*), Patty Duke was not earning points for good behavior. However, the story has a happy ending. In 1972 Patty married an actor named John Astin, who had played a ghoulish character, Gomez, in the monstrous television series "The Addams Family." They made a number of TV appearances together, became domestic, and at last report were happily raising a large family.

The point about the Patty Duke story is that all the details of her private life not only were allowed to become public but also were given wide publicity. That was quite a change for Hollywood. Where audiences once were not allowed to have a hint that Judy Garland might possibly be having a bit of trouble with pills, moviegoers, and television viewers today are diligently fed every bit of information about their stars' private lives, no matter how young those stars might happen to be. And more than that, child stars today are playing roles that Hollywood once thought would be forbidden even for the toughest adult stars.

Take Brooke Shields, who was a beauty queen in Hollywood by the time she was twelve years old. In a movie called *King of the Gypsies* Brooke played a young girl who was forced into an arranged marriage by a gypsy tribe—and that was about the most mentionable of the parts she played even before she was a teenager. In the Hollywood of old, the topic of drug addiction was simply not mentioned on the screen. But in the new Hollywood, a young black actor named Larry B. Scott played a thirteen-year-old heroin addict in a 1978 film, *A Hero Ain't Nothin' But a Sandwich.* The audience could watch Larry inject the drug into his arm, and Larry—who was actually an active member of a church—gave interviews describing the drug life on city streets.

It was getting so that child stars would hardly be allowed to attend some of the movies they made. All the old stardust had been knocked off the characters, leaving, it seemed, no innocence behind. In the old Hollywood, a movie about kids and baseball was pure idealism, which always ended with the hero getting the big hit that knocked in the winning run. In the new scheme of things, a baseball film was something else; Larry Scott, for example, starred in a TV movie called *The Rag Tag Champs*, in which he played a Little League third baseman whose parents had deserted him. In *The Bad News Bears* (1976), a comedy about kid baseball players, one outstanding feature was the foul language—the kind of language that once was forbidden in any Hollywood movie, let alone a film with kids in it. Nevertheless, the film spawned a sequel, *The Bad News Bears in Breaking Training* (1977), showing that audiences would accept that sort of talk from kids.

Audiences, it seemed, would accept almost anything from kids. The clean, wholesome, middle-class atmosphere of "Father Knows Best" was replaced on television by the slouching, sloppy teenagers of a run-down Brooklyn high school, led by a tender-hearted but tough teacher in "Welcome Back, Kotter." Every old Hollywood cliché was shattered by this one show. Its group of teenagers included a Puerto Rican Jew, Juan Epstein; an Italian braggart, Vinnie Barbarino; a proud black, Freddie Washington; and another character, Arnold Horschack, who simply did not fit in any of the old movie characterizations. Even their casual banter —"Up your nose with a rubber hose"—would have sent an old-time Hollywood mogul out of a screening room in terror, determined to kill the whole project.

The TV audience could also watch "Good Times," a comedy series starring a black comedian, Jimmy Walker, playing

The 1970s image of the American teenager: John Travolta in *Saturday Night Fever*. (Paramount, 1977)

a teenager in a ghetto family. This was no Andy Hardy world with clean, big houses and immaculate lawns. Instead, the series had the Evans family living in an apartment, and young J.J. was up against all the problems of the real world—unemployment, eviction, crime, and all the rest. Once upon a TV time, the fact that the teenagers in "Father Knows Best" had to grapple with problems like the senior prom and getting a date for Saturday night was regarded as a major step forward in reality. But J.J. on "Good Times" had to shoulder new responsibilities when his father died, and one episode before that featured a mugging. The situations still were played for laughs, but the world of the American teenager had become a lot less innocent than it had been just a few decades earlier.

And the world of the screen tot had become equally sophisticated in the 1970s, as the story of Tatum O'Neal showed vividly. Both off and on the screen, innocence was out of style. On the screen, nine-year-old Tatum (she was named after her mother's grandmother) made her debut as a cigarette-smoking, prematurely wise assistant to a traveling con man in the 1973 film *Paper Moon*. Shirley Temple sang and danced her way into the hearts of Americans by radiating nothing but sweetness. Tatum O'Neal became the biggest child star in the new Hollywood by lying and cheating her way through life, faithful only to the swindler—her father, Ryan O'Neal—who had picked her up.

Off the screen, the situation was even more horrendous by 1930s standards. To start with, everyone cheerfully acknowledged that Tatum's parents were divorced—a marital status that was perfectly acceptable in the 1970s but was unthinkable in the 1930s. (Some film buffs may remember a fast-talking 1938 comedy called *Boy Meets Girl,* set in a Hollywood film studio, in which the fate of a baby star rises or falls on whether the child's parents were married; Jimmy Cagney and Pat O'Brien brightened that film.) In addition, Tatum's father also acknowledged in interviews that his daughter was anything but a perfect student; she was expelled from a private school just before the *Paper Moon* part of Addie Loggins came along.

True, Tatum was discovered somewhat in classic Hollywood style, but even the discovery was not as uncalculated as it once had been. Tatum was visiting her father on the set of one of his films, *The Thief Who Came to Dinner* (typically, the movie had Ryan O'Neal playing a jewel thief who got away with it, thwarting an honest cop). She was noticed by the wife of a rising young director named Peter Bogdanovich. A few months later, Bogdanovich went over to the O'Neal house to see Tatum, who supposedly knew nothing about a possible movie role. As soon as he walked in the house, Tatum asked, "Is this the guy who's going to direct the movie?" She got the part anyway.

Once upon a time, it was standard for everyone who worked with a child star to have nothing but praise for the kid's hard work and intelligence. Any indication that the kid needed help in acting, or that the star's behavior was less than perfect, was avoided. But Bogdanovich, in the new atmosphere of the 1970s, admitted freely that he had spent long hours coaching Tatum (she had never had an acting lesson) and that he had helped her get her lines right by

Tatum O'Neal and her father, Ryan O'Neal, in her first movie and biggest hit, *Paper Moon*. (Paramount, 1973)

offering her bribes that started out at fifty cents and ended at fifty dollars.

The coaching and the bribery—and Tatum's natural talent —all paid off. She won an Academy Award, and the movie made more than $45 million at the box office. Ryan O'Neal hadn't thought about more than one film for his daughter, but the offers were so good that they couldn't be resisted, especially when Tatum began to learn what money could buy. Soon Tatum was both famous and rich, and having her share of publicity.

It wasn't the old kind of child-star publicity, which was heavy on gingham dresses and ice cream cones. Tatum O'Neal was part of the jet set. She was seen in swank discotheques, dancing with her father. She was interviewed by Andy Warhol. She went shopping in London, was photographed for *Vogue* magazine, drove around in a Mercedes, made the night-club scene. She fought with costar Walter Matthau on the set of *The Bad News Bears*, although they ended as friends. She acknowledged that she had secretly been smoking cigarettes for three years before her role in *Paper Moon*. In short, she was the very model of a 1970s child star, a million light years away from the old innocent stereotype. In 1978 Tatum was in England to film *International Velvet*, a sequel to Elizabeth Taylor's big 1944 hit, *National Velvet*.

Tatum was just thirteen years old and at the top of the world. (She wasn't allowed to take a fall off a horse in the film because the insurance company wouldn't allow it; an ex-jockey doubled for her.) She was making just one film a year, trying to live a fairly normal life when she went to high school in California between roles—and rapidly approaching the time of life when most child stars face their greatest challenge, growing up. No one could tell what the future would bring Tatum O'Neal.

And no one could tell who the next big child star would be. In 1978 there was ten-year-old Quinn Cummings, who won an Oscar nomination for her role as a saucy little girl in the Neil Simon comedy *The Goodbye Girl*. Quinn was definitely a child of the television age. She started out in commercials (Future floor wax and Pop Tarts among other products), played in a short-lived comedy series, "Big Eddie," acted in such series as "The Six Million Dollar Man," and was on the set of "Baretta" when she was told of her Academy Award nomination.

Not only that: Quinn Cummings rides in a Jaguar, appears casually on "The Johnny Carson Show," and reacted scornfully when she was told that Margaret O'Brien's aunt used to get movie tears out of her by telling her that her dog had died. "I don't think something like that could have fooled me," she told a reporter.

Some of the old things, like the tradition of sweetness and light that goes back to Mary Pickford, have obviously changed. But most of the old dreams still remain alive. Who knows—perhaps the next big child star will flash before your eyes tonight on television. Maybe it's that baby who is having his diapers changed. Or maybe it's a kid who is out in Hollywood, trying out for that big chance on the silver screen: The old dream about being discovered in a drug store and going on to become the world-famous star, driving around in a Rolls Royce and having people ask for your autograph, still exists.

And just maybe (perish the thought, don't let it interfere with your studying tomorrow's lessons or doing your geography homework, and don't think that it can happen without hard work and a lot of good luck and an unusually good break) but just maybe—it could be you.

A postscript: When you have those dreams of glory, it's well to remember Bobby Breen, the curly-haired singing star of the 1930s. Bobby was discovered by Eddie Cantor, the comedian, and became a star with his first film, *Let's Sing Again* (1936). Soon you could hear him on all the big radio shows and watch him in movie after movie. Bobby's young soprano, invariably described as "sweet," was the key to his success; when he opened in a 1937 movie titled *Make a Wish*, one reviewer noted sourly that Bobby "exudes sweetness all over the screen to an annoying degree" and that he "sings like an angel but he acts like the devil."

Despite the complaints, the money rolled in (and was thoughtfully put away in a trust fund by Bobby's sister Sally). Then Bobby Breen turned twelve, and his voice changed.

Thirty years later, Bobby Breen was still making comebacks.

INDEX

Gable, Clark, 10, 15, 17, 83
Garbo, Greta, 10, 42, 57
Garfield, John, 74
Garland, Judy, 9, 16–20, 22, 23, 25, 32, 33, 45, 69, 82, 110
Garner, Peggy Ann, 35–36, 45
Garson, Greer, 30, 33
Gilchrist, John, 98–99
Gorcey, Bernard, 75, 77
Gorcey, Leo, 74–76, 77
Grable, Betty, 38
Grant, Cary, 14, 29, 46
Granville, Bonita (Mrs. John Wrather), 77–80, 83, 106
Gray, Billy, 101
Great Expectations, 80, 84
Gypsy, 89, 90

Hall, Huntz, 74–76, 77
Harlow, Jean, 15
Harris, Julie, 50
Hayward, Susan, 35
Hepburn, Katharine, 10, 28
Hickman, Darryl, 83
Hickman, Dwayne, 105
Hitler's Children, 78, 79
Homeier, Skip, 79
Hood, Darla, 62
Hoskins, Allen ("Farina"), 55, 56, 57, 62–63
Howard, Ron, 102
Human Comedy, The, 23, 47

Jane Eyre, 33, 87
Jean, Gloria (Gloria Jean Schoonover), . . . 71–72
Jenkins, Butch, 47–48
Johnson, Van, 47, 82
Jolson Story, The, 58, 59, 83
Jones, Dean, 96
Jordan, Bobby, 75

Kaye, Darwood, 63
Kelly, Gene, 50, 90
Kerry, Margaret, 30–31
Kid, The, 37–38, 39
Kidnapped, 44, 60
Kilburn, Terry, 83
Kornman, Mary, 55, 56, 58–60

Lahr, Bert, 18
Lamont, Charles, 11
Lassie Come Home, 87, 92, 93
Lee, Porky, 63
Le Roy, Baby, 4
Little Lord Fauntelroy, 42–44, 68
Little Miss Marker, 14
Little Nellie Kelly, 20
"Little Rascals, The," 54, 65
Lolita, 96
Lydon, Jimmy, 73
Lynch, Peggy, 30–31

McCormack, Patty, 106–9
McDowall, Roddy, 92–94
McFarland, George ("Spanky"), 57, 60–62
McGowan, Robert, 64
McLaglen, Victor, 42
MacMurray, Fred, 35, 60–62, 83, 90
Madame Curie, 33, 34
Maid of Salem, 79
Mathers, Jerry, 103, 105
Matthau, Walter, 116
Meet Me in St. Louis, 32, 33
Member of the Wedding, The, 5, 49, 50
Midsummer Night's Dream, A, 21
Mills, Hayley, 94, 95–96
Minnelli, Liza, 82, 84
Mineo, Sal, 90
Miracle on 34th Street, 90, 91
Miracle Worker, The, 109
Miss Annie Rooney, 5
Monroe, Marilyn, 46, 105
Moore, Dickie, 5–7, 57
Morrison, Ernie ("Sunshine Sammy"), 56, 57
My Brother Talks to Horses, 47

National Velvet, 30, 47, 87, 88, 116
Newman, Paul, 49
Niven, David, 34
North, Jay, 103–5

O'Brien, Margaret, 31–34, 35, 47, 48, 50, 117
O'Brien, Pat, 45, 114
Oliver Twist, 5, 38

Author Biography

EDWARD EDELSON spends most of his working hours as the science editor of the New York *Daily News,* but he still manages to find the time to watch plenty of movies. A graduate of New York University and a Sloan-Rockefeller Fellow in the Advanced Science Writing Program at Columbia University, Mr. Edelson now lives in Jamaica, New York, with his wife and three children. His previous books include *Great Monsters of the Movies, The Book of Prophecy, Visions of Tomorrow, Funny Men of the Movies, Great Movie Spectaculars,* and *Tough Guys and Gals of Movies.*

LIBRARY
LONGFELLOW SCHOOL
BERKELEY, CALIF.